I0165315

1

Buttermilk Book Publishing

Myrtle Beach, South Carolina

Copyright T. Allen Winn 2020

All Rights Reserved

This is a work of fiction. Storyline and characters are fictitious and originated from the imagination of the author.

Typecast in Times New Roman

ISBN 978-1-7331576-6-7

Come Here Getouttahere, Tyler's Tail Wagging Tale

Chapters

Properly trained, a man can be dog's best friend.

Scratch a dog and you'll find a permanent job.

Man is a dog's idea of what God should be.

If dogs could talk, it would take a lot of the fun out of owning one.

Anybody who doesn't know what soap tastes like never washed a dog.

A door is what a dog is perpetually on the wrong side of.

If your dog is fat, you're not getting enough exercise.

I wonder what goes through his mind when he sees us peeing in his water bowl.

I wonder if other dogs think poodles are members of a weird religious cult.

I am not your dog, but if every time you saw me, you gave me a backrub, I would run to greet you, too.

A dog has so many friends because it wags its tail instead of its tongue.

Dogs laugh, but they laugh with their tails.

Dogs are really people with short legs in fur coats.

The more I see of man, the more I like dogs - my goal in life is to be as good of a person my dog already thinks I am.

A cat, after being scolded, goes about its business. A dog slinks off into a corner and pretends to be doing a serious self-reappraisal.

If you think dogs can't count, try putting three dog biscuits in your pocket and then giving him only two of them.

If you want the best seat in the house ... move the dog.

Chasing your tail gets you nowhere, except back to where you started.

Life is just one table scrap after another, when please doesn't work ... Beg.

You might be barking up the wrong tree if you think a barking dog never bites.

Dogs are not our whole life, but they make our lives whole.

Properly trained, a man can be dog's best friend.

Adults tend to reflect as we get older. I'm no different. It's usually better to think about the good times past than the bad one's present. But we don't always have complete control over our thoughts. Thankfully I'm in one of those good nostalgic moods, one from my childhood, memories of Papa, those times we shared, bonding as only a grandkid and granddad can. Who knows what triggers these moments? Sometimes they just happen. When they do, I just go with the flow.

Daydreams or nightdreams, one is just as good as the other. Daydreams might be a tad better, as Papa might say. You have a bit more control over them and you're not likely to forget important details as what often happens when you wake from your slumber. For now, I'm just going to ride the wave and cherish the moment.

The 1960's were vintage years for a boy growing up in the south. Times were simple as was life. You had time to breath it all in and cherish family tradition. The chaos of today is consumed by people too focused on themselves, taking selfies, sending text messages instead of having normal face to face conversations. Those of today are spoiled and sadly the center of their universe.

Give it a couple of more generations and humanity will have forgotten how to talk and socialize. Technology is okay in small doses but today it is as addictive as any drug. Right now, I'm back in 1961 and away from a world spinning out of control. As old folks say, 'it is almost like yesterday.' This is my journey, my story, how it happened as far as my memory will allow.

Papa sat on the front porch, like he did most every weekday afternoon, sipping a glass of ice-cold tea, sweet tea that is, southern style. The evening sun had a few hours yet to go before giving up to the invading twilight. He had finished most of his daily chores, all except for making that final walk through his vegetable garden just before darkness snuffed out the last tad of daylight. He sported a well-worn grey fedora and his faded denim overalls over a white cotton tee-shirt. His wardrobe seldom changed, except on Sundays when he broke out his blue suit, white button-down shirt and polka dotted black and white bowtie. He called this his prayer meeting getup, his Sunday's best.

Granny made sure he attended, saying weekdays were for gardening, painting, fishing and hunting, but the Sabbath belonged to the Lord and his faithful flock. Faithful could be debatable but Papa was raised to be a God-fearing man. He respected Granny's wishes and treated Sundays with sincere reverence.

I just so happened to be spending the week with my grandparents, something I did quite often. Nine years old, no kicking and screaming from me, I looked forward to staying with them, especially when school was out, like it was right now. My summer reprieve from incarceration had just begun and I didn't plan to squander a single minute of my former imprisonment. Well, school isn't really prison but to each his own interpretation. I thrive on drama. There's nothing wrong with having a vivid imagination, or so says Papa when it's just me and him paling around. Just between us men folk is how he likes to put it.

Shirtless, barefooted and with my cut off blue jeans, we made a fine pair sitting in that porch swing, sipping our sweet tea and chewing the fat. I had already helped him with his manly chores, feeding the chickens, tending to the one milk cow and weeding the garden. We had even taken time off with good behavior to have us a big ole bowl of orange sherbet. Granny had brought it to us under the shade tree in the backyard. We had washed it down with an RC Cola. Summers were perfect as always.

An adult, now looking back, times were much simpler when I didn't have to deal with the rat race I live in today. Peter Pan had it right, never wanting to grow up. Dealing with only three television channels, instead of a zillion and getting it free, made for a more laid-back life. There was something special, almost scientific about adjusting and redirecting those rabbit ears to zoom in on a static free picture on the tube. Adding tin foil to the tips of the rabbit ears was some sort of miracle amplifier. I was the remote control, my parents or grandparents sending me to the TV to change the channels. I didn't argue about my task. It was understood, just part of watching television, our abbreviated version of channel surfing. I got my exercise. They were the certified couch potatoes before the term had become popular.

For many years I even helped Papa draw water from a well. That's before they got city water piped to where they lived in the country. It didn't come all prepackaged in bottles and it was free. Nothing is free now, that's for sure. Everything comes with a cost attached to it. I didn't know just how I had it made back then, a time before everything came out of my paycheck. The only bathroom was outside instead of inside. It was a two-seater outhouse. I'm not sure why it had two holes instead of one, nothing separating them for privacy. I don't recall ever having company while I used it. The little shed had a simple hook and latch inside to secure your privacy. If it was locked, it was occupied. I never saw any lines waiting their turn.

Yep, here we sit, two peas in a pod, sipping our sweet tea. Occasionally we swished and jingled the ice cubes in the glass to keep the cold evenly distributed. Ice was bought and then stored in a refrigerated ice chest. And a glass might be stretching the truth just a bit. Granny used emptied out and washed squeaky clean glass grape jelly jars. Back then you didn't throw away good stuff that could be used for something else. She had a table setting for ten or twelve people. The men of the family got to use quart sized mason jars on Sundays because it took less refilling for their thirsty souls.

Coffee and lard cans, anything that came in tin plates, were all utilized in some form or fashion. Tinfoil could even be reused almost forever. Folks back then were recycling before the term had been invented. An aunt of mine even washed and reused plastic plates, cups and utensils. We didn't have to worry about dishwasher safe because people washed the dishes, not machines. I like thinking back to those days.

My life was full of firsts, magical moments, unpredictable scenarios with unquestionable family love and care. We sat at a table and ate our meals, no disruptions from television or any other electronic devices. We talked, laughed and reminisced, all without the aid of gadgets. If the phone rang, we answered it. There were no answering machines, call waiting or forwarding; well, unless you had a party line shared with the neighbors. You dialed and didn't mash buttons or tell the phone to call somebody.

We possessed social skills, unlike the up and coming generation of today, some texting one another from less than ten feet away. My rules today, no technology is allowed at the dining room table. Live by this rule while you eat at my table or risk losing your phones all together. And, we will eat as a family always should, together, same time, same meals, not fragmented and scattered about.

Papa, my knight in shining denim, sat beside me in the old cedar swing. The chain made those odd creaking noises, not a squeak that needs oiling but more of a comforting sound, hard to describe unless you were on the porch with us. There's nothing like the men folk sharing a shady spot after a hard day's work, talking up stuff like drowning some red wigglers and wetting hooks in the favorite fishing hole. What I wouldn't do to have Papa and those cherished moments back.

Papa, dead and buried some ten years ago now but I still have those vivid memories to this very day. Papa first spotted the approaching varmint before I did. To him everything fury and four legged was a varmint; mostly good for nothing to hear him tell it. He didn't latch on too fondly to any critters that didn't serve a purpose. Chickens were two legged but were at least egg producers and edible if you so took a notion.

Cats, even those pesky strays, kept down the rat and snake population. The cow gave us milk, butter and cheese and was edible as well. We never ate his cows though. A good mule was worth its weight in gold; at least when hitched to a plow or a wagon. Dogs, unless they were hunting hounds, rabbit chasing beagles or just a mean watch dog, had no place on his property. Strays beware.

The dog made the grave mistake of venturing into the yard, Papa's domain, territory it had no business in. The encroacher was midsized with jet black shiny short hair. It had a long snout with one ear standing up and the other one floppy, like maybe it was broken. It's long rat like tail was tucked low. I had never seen it before and if Papa had, he didn't mention it. Papa usually called dogs like this 'Sooners', a mixed breed, a mutt, a mongrel, not good for anything but eating and pooping.

The dog crept along the hedgerow and hadn't taken notice of us. Papa had stopped the swing, anchoring it with both feet touching the porch. He watched to see just what the no-good varmint was up to in his yard. The dog paused and hiked his leg on the fig bush. I glanced over at him and knew instantly that the stuff that hits the fan was about to fly. He stood up, leaving me and my dangling feet alone in the swing.

Papa patted his side noisily with his hand while stomping his foot, a little attention getter for the trespasser. The dog stopped dead in its tracks and looked our way. Instead of tucking his tail and running like most did when Papa called them out, it rolled out its tongue, almost looking to be smiling as it wagged a friendly tail. This made Papa furious. How dare the interloper react in such a manner and not be hauling tail instead.

Papa pretended to throw something at it. The dog slowed its tail wagging and cocked its head as if to say, 'you really didn't throw anything, did you?' Papa was now fit to be tied. This was his yard and no varmint was about to disrespect him here. He stomped his foot harder and louder, clapping his hands for special effects.

The dog cocked its head one way and then the other before then promptly lying down. Papa had not given it the command to lie down. I cringed, hoping the dog wouldn't voluntarily roll over or stand on its hind legs to worsen matters. It didn't. It just waited and watched.

I again made the mistake of looking at Papa. His face was red, beet red as he might describe it. I could have sworn I saw steam coming from his ears but remember I'm the one with the wild imagination. The jig was up. Papa walked to the edge of the porch, a mere eight steps from ground level and within rock throwing distance of the ill-mannered varmint, if he would have had a real rock. The dog flicked its one good ear, still appearing to just stay put and smile back at us.

Papa yelled, 'Get-outta-here.' It didn't, so he yelled it two more times, giving it a combined hand clap and foot stomp. The way he shouted, it sounded like one long word as only a true southerner can phrase it. 'Getouttahere', he yelled even louder, a scary tone from where I sat motionless behind him in that swing.

The Sooner was apparently practicing the creed of being man's best friend or it was deaf, dumb, stupid or fearless. Papa was anything but in a friendly mood. He didn't take too kindly to being upstaged by the fury four-legged foe. The dog seemed determined to convince him otherwise.

A part of me wanted to speak up and tell Papa that maybe the dog didn't have a home or was hungry or something. The smart part of me told me to keep my mouth shut and my nose out of his business. Kids are not really known for keeping quiet though. Words tend to bypass our brain and go directly to our mouth. I guess that's where that saying originated, 'from the mouths of babes.'

Television host, Art Linkletter might say, 'Kids say the darndest things.' I loved that TV show called *Kids Say the Darndest Things*. I could have easily been one of those kids saying the darndest things. Would Papa appreciate it now though was the million-dollar question. He hadn't exactly asked me for my opinion on the matter. The dog just continued to lie there. Papa was now standing two steps below the porch, still yelling *getouttahere, you hear me, you mangy flea-bitten mutt.*

I was tempted to sprint past Papa and go pet the friendly dog. I love animals, especially dogs. There was something about this one that screamed *can't we all be best friends.* Papa wasn't in a friendly state of mind. He wanted this trespasser out of his yard, the sooner the better.

How many more times was he going to yell *getouttahere* was anyone's guess? I had already lost count. Papa descended two more steps. The dog sat up, tail still mildly wagging. It panted, his tongue lollygagging about, inviting Papa to come on down. I feared for what Papa might do if the dog stood its ground. It wasn't going anywhere so it appeared.

Maybe it was sick or hurt. It didn't look sick or hurt but what did I really know about dog looks. I had never had one for a pet. I hadn't ever thought about it. Maybe I was thinking about it a little at this moment though. The dog might already have a home nearby. Plus, Papa would never give in to my silly notion for a good for nothing worthless fleabag as he often called strays.

He had reached the bottom step, now even with the stone sidewalk he had made himself. He shouted one more *getouttahere* for good measure, but the dog only stood, still wagging his tail, tongue wagging almost as much, that one ear perked up and flicking.

Papa reached down and picked up a rock, half the size of a potato. Without giving it much thought, I was quickly out of the swing and down the steps just as Papa drew back his arm. To this day I don't know where I had gotten the guts to do what I did. I grabbed Papa by his stout forearm with both of my tiny hands. He stopped in mid throw, not that I had overpowered him even by the stretch of my vivid imagination.

He asked me, 'What's the matter son?' I could have easily lifted my feet from the ground and swung from his arm, but I didn't, not this time. I spoke my mind. Papa said honest men spoke their mind, right, wrong or indifferent. I sure hoped he appreciated me speaking mine.

It was too late to back track. That was for sure. I half asked and half begged him not to hurt the dog. Papa eyed me man to boy and then redirected his look at the dog. It was still just standing there with its entire body wagging about as if it was infested with wiggle worms.

20

Judgment day had arrived. Would he or wouldn't he throw the rock? He still gripped his projectile and he couldn't possibly miss at this distance unless he wished to miss. Time was at an ultimate standstill. I was in one of those slow-motion movie sequences, so my imagination directed me.

"What is it to you son that I spare this good for nothing mangy varmint?"

Now he was looking for me to come up with a reason. I hadn't really given that any thought. My imagination ruled, but nobody ever asked me to toss in my two cents worth. Most would consider my input as not being worth a plug nickel. I was just a kid. I wasn't smart enough to know worldly things yet.

He stood there patiently waiting for me to answer him, all the while he palmed and then re-gripped his weapon of choice. The dog appeared to be waiting for my reply too. Too much hinged on me saying the right thing; way too much pressure for a nine-year-old boy to endure.

"Papa, maybe the varmint needs a new best friend."

That sounded even more stupid after it passed through my lips. It's better when I keep that stuff inside my head and not for the world to hear. I never learn.

"Son, are you telling me that you want this fleabag? You've never owned a dog. You've never mentioned to me ever wanting to have a dog. What do you even know about what it takes to own a dog?"

Boy, for one simple answer, Papa was sure firing back a lot of questions and stuff at me. Without thinking, which is a bad idea from the get-go, I blurted out an answer, "He can train me."

"Did I just hear you right, boy? You are going to let that worthless hound train you to be its best friend, the dog's master."

That sounded even crazier coming out of Papa's mouth than it had mine. Had I really just said that? Was the dog buying it any better than Papa? One must live with the consequences, so said my mama. I had said it, stupid or not. I must now somehow be convincing and live with the consequences. Hindsight, I should have just stayed in the swing and kept my nose out of Papa's business.

"Yes sir, who says a dog can't train people to be there best friend? Look at him, Papa.

He's all but taught us not to throw rocks at him."

"I reckon he has at that with a little help from you. Let's just suppose I convince your grandma and then your folks to let you keep him; do you promise me right here and now that you will take care of him?"

"I promise you we will take care of each other."

"I'm beginning to think that varmint has some sort of magical spell cast over you."

"Us, you mean, Papa, you didn't hit him with that rock."

"The Sooner needs a name. What will it be, boy?"

Sometimes my imagination just gets the best of me. Without much thought at all I blurted out an even worse answer than the last one. "We can call him, Getouttahere."

"You want him to stay or leave? Make up your mind."

I squatted and said, "Come here, Getouttahere." And he did.

"Well I'll be a monkey's uncle. All this time I've been saying that and now look at this critter doing the opposite. It must be some kind of sign."

He dropped his rock and then patted the mangy, good for nothing, varmint on the head. Getouttahere had some mighty powerful training skills, so it seemed. He had enchanted Papa, something I had never witnessed. Papa seemed to be just as confounded by his actions concerning the varmint.

Scratch a dog and you'll
find a permanent job.

Papa had done what he said he would do and had convinced everyone to give me a shot at having a dog. Now I needed to convince the dog. So far, he came when I called but I wasn't sure he really knew his name was Getouttahere. What if someone like Papa was yelling at him to get out of here and instead, he came to them? I was having second thoughts about my name choice, but my wild imagination wasn't coming up with anything different. My bad, he already looked like Getouttahere. The name stands, I suppose.

Now I was faced with challenges. As Papa had pointed out, what did I really know about taking care of a dog, any animal as far as that goes? I'd never had a pet. Well I did have a goldfish once. I was just a kid then. I seem to remember it getting flushed down the toilet, not much of a funeral for a belly-up fish.

My friend Frankie blamed me for its death saying I had overfed it. He had called me a fish murderer. Friends can be so cruel. I lived with that guilt for at least a week. Maybe that's why I never asked to have another pet. Yep, it was Frankie's fault. I'll show him this time, I hoped.

First things first, my daddy said we'd have to take Getouttahere to the Vet to make sure he was healthy. That made me feel much better, having my dog looked at by an animal doctor. It would be tough to flush a dog. The doctor gave him all kinds of shots, rabies, worms, and distemper.

He didn't seem to have a temper to me. I asked daddy why he needed a temper shot. He said, 'No silly, not temper, distemper.' This temper, that temper, what did I really know about temper medication. He then spelled it for me and explained that the doctor had told him that distemper was the leading cause of infectious disease death in dogs. Dogs could get a high fever, runny nose and throw up a lot.

I sure needed no help in killing my pets. Just ask Frankie. Worms can kill dogs too. I wondered if you could fish with dog worms. I'd have to ask Papa that one. Rabies made you crazy. I had seen movies about people foaming at the mouth and turning into raving monsters.

Getouttahere left the doctor's office with a clean bill of health, so said my daddy. That meant no worries of worms, his temper or rabies. If anything happened to my dog from here on out it would be pinned on me for sure. Frankie would be the first one to point a finger.

I wondered if they had a 'How to Book' at the library to explain taking care of a pet dog. I had vowed that my dog would be the teacher. I hoped he was a good teacher. Never mind, I'd just ask Papa. He knew everything about everything. I had never asked him a question that he didn't have an answer for what I was asking.

Granny once told me to not believe everything he told me. Liar, liar, pants on fire…I don't think he would ever lie to me. Frankie would though. He drew pleasure from yanking my chain. My chain must be easy to yank because he sure pulled the wool over my eyes more times than I can count. Mama called it being too gullible and trusting. Frankie would just say *never trust a fish murderer*. I sure didn't want to be known as a dog killer.

I better learn this taking care of thing real fast. Frankie had all sorts of advice, but I didn't trust most of what he told me. I have a wild imagination, but I think Frankie just plain makes stuff up. I believe he believes most of what comes out of his mouth. He does have a dog, so I reckon he's more of an expert than me. He's never had to flush his.

Boy, I didn't know so much stuff had to be done to have a dog. We had to make sure Getouttahere had a water dish and a food dish. I'm not as big and strong as Frankie so handling that big bag of dry dog food was not easy. Papa saw me struggling with it and said, *son, try this instead.* He gave me a plastic cup and told me to just scoop out what I needed instead of trying to boy-handle the giant bag.

We bought Getouttahere a collar with a dog tag that had his name and address on it. I wondered why kids didn't have to wear them too. It would sure make it a lot easier if we got lost and couldn't remember our house address.

We got him a long leash too. I hadn't tried that out yet. We had to find a place for him to sleep. Mama had already put her foot down, telling me he absolutely would not sleep in my bed. Heck, I hadn't even thought of him sleeping in my bed until she said that. My fish had never slept in my bed. Why would I think a dog would sleep there? Hey, I was new at this pet owner stuff, if you didn't count the goldfish.

I did learn one think very quickly though or maybe Getouttahere was just an excellent trainer. Dogs do love to be scratched. I love a good back scratching come to think of it but most of the time I only scratch myself when I have an itch. Itches can pop up most anywhere on your body. Mama fusses at me sometimes saying *don't scratch there when you're in a public place.* She doesn't understand that itches can happen even in public places, and an unscratched itch is not a happy itch.

Dogs must itch all the time. They are forever scratching. The only thing better to them is if you help with the scratching. Getouttahere doesn't really care where I scratch him, just so long as I do. I don't think there even has to be an itch involved. Be warned though, once you start scratching a dog, stopping is tougher than starting.

It can be a fulltime job scratching a dog. Your arms and hands will grow tired before a dog is ready for you to quit. Getouttahere will nudge or paw my hand when I try to stop. He likes putting the guilt trip on me, looking at me with what else but his puppy dog droopy eyes. Mama sometimes warns me to not look at her with my puppy dog eyes when I really want something badly. I can't remember if I learned that from Getouttahere or if he learned it from me. I do know it works most of the time.

I first thought he must have fleas because he scratched so much or wanted to be scratched. No dog could have that many fleas though. Besides, the Vet dipped him in medicine to supposedly kill all the fleas and ticks. Worms, fleas, ticks…what else likes chomping on dogs?

Ear scratching, you better never start doing that unless you have all the time in the world. Getouttahere will turn his head one way and then the other; sometimes his back leg will start twitching and scratching too while I'm scratching him. It can be a real job.

Sometimes I regret ever learning about how he liked it. I wish the Vet would have given him an anti-itch shot. Sometimes dogs have things wrong with them that make them itch, so says Frankie, the know-it-all. He just likes to make me worry about stuff. The Vet had given him an A-Okay check-up, so I tried to tune out Frankie.

Getouttahere didn't self scratch that much. He liked me doing it. That told me he wasn't sick. I'm smarter than I look. Frankie would argue that fact. For now, the scratching routine was boy-dog bonding just between us men folks so would say Papa.

Man is a dog's idea of
what God should be.

Reminiscing of having my very first dog was sort of an eye-opening experience even all these years later. It was easy to see the wrong and right things I did when playing them through my head now. The learning curve had been quite steep for one who had never been a real pet owner. I don't think having one goldfish really meets the pet owner guidelines and qualifications.

What I've learned now, being a wiser old coot, is that dogs are really pack animals, descendants of wolves. In every pack there must be the Alpha male, the leader, and dogs look for that leadership. If the human doesn't choose to be the leader then the dog will assume that responsibility. How many times do you hear about the dog being spoiled, getting everything, it wants and basically taking charge of the household?

A person not stepping up to be the pack leader allows this to happen, so say the experts. No, this didn't come from Frankie. I haven't seen him in over forty years. But thinking back now, I can almost visualize its impact.

Getouttahere and I were doing just fine. Well, I guess I can't really speak for him. At least he wasn't complaining about anything I was doing, if I was doing anything wrong or anything that didn't suit him. We were inseparable, joined at the hips, Papa would say. We did go just about everywhere together, or everywhere my folks would allow.

Mama had softened up a tad. He was even allowed to occasionally sleep with me. Well, maybe more than occasionally. Mama didn't necessarily have to know everything. A boy and his dog must keep some secrets.

Frankie said it was more like a dog with his boy, but he just said that to get under my skin. Most of the time it did just that. Frankie was too good at pushing my button. What are friends for, right? I really think he was just a bit jealous of my dog. After all, he had been about my only real friend before Getouttahere came along. That's all right, let him be. He had dished out enough junk to me that he deserved being on the short end of the stick for a change.

Getouttahere depended on me for most everything, food, water, letting him in, letting him out. Papa said it was important to remember who runs the show; and remind the sooner of that fact. He acted like he didn't like Getouttahere but I could tell he really did. He couldn't fool me.

Papa was an old softy, but he would never lay claim to any such notion. At his house, he ruled the roost; that is unless Granny had her say so in the matter. A rooster can be henpecked.

In Papa's world men were the providers, the bread winners, the masters of the household. All major decisions were made by him. Granny said she allowed him to think that way. Mama backed her up quoting some famous saying that behind every successful man was a woman. I wondered where that left me standing in the pecking order. Maybe behind every successful boy is his dog. Getouttahere would probably back me on that.

Frankie said that dogs worshipped their masters. I didn't really feel like a master. I felt like a boy that had a dog for his best friend. Frankie always had some sort of wise crack about everything. He stuck by his convictions that we were lord and masters of the universe when it came to having any pet. I couldn't help but wonder if pets saw us that way, as some sort of god. I certainly didn't want that job, even though Frankie put up a good argument.

He would say stuff like what would a dog do without us. They depended on us for their food. While they could lap up water most anyplace and did, we provided fresh water just the same. We made sure they had a place to sleep and took care of them when they were sick. Right, and flushed them down the toilet. Like I said before, Frankie had a chance to say it.

Frankie stuck to his guns when it came to this master stuff. He said we made sure they were kept warm and did our best to keep them cool. Dogs pant all the time so who could really be sure about that last one. Lord and master so said Frankie, but did Getouttahere really look at me as being a dog god?

Dogs didn't go to church or read bibles so why did they need a god-like person in their lives? I blew off Frankie and his silly babbling and decided to take it to a reliable source, Papa. He knew everything. He'd have all the right answers. Remembering to remember to ask him, there lay the problem.

Sometimes I even surprise myself. I did remember the next time I was around Papa. I asked him straight up; did dogs look up to us as gods? We were sitting out back under the old oak shade tree, sipping a cold iced tea in grape jelly jars when I posed the question. He rubbed his chin for a second, set his iced tea down on an old hickory stump used for chopping up wood and splitting kindling. He then slid his thumbs through the suspenders of his overalls. He sort of rocked backwards and forward for a second before answering. He told me that there was only one God and dogs weren't smart enough to know that or think that we were Him.

Papa insisted that we were the dog's master though, not to be confused with being a dog's god. I asked him how he really knew what a dog thought. It seemed like a reasonable question to me. He told me that dogs don't think. They just do what we tell them to do; most of the time, anyway he added.

He eventually ended the conversation, if my listening and him talking is really a conversation, by telling me not to fret over it. He said a dog needed us more that we needed it. He pointed out how much simpler my life had been before the fleabag had weaseled its way into it. Papa quickly pointed out that now that I was in the dog's life, the dog couldn't do without me.

My mouth doesn't know when to stay shut. I asked him, 'Then doesn't that sort of make me the dog's god?' He took a big swig of tea after that one and simply replied, No. The conversation was over whether I wanted it to be or not.

I wasn't sure if I was any closer to the answer, but I decided to go with Papa's notion over Frankie's. He was, after all, older and wiser. What did a couple of nine-year, almost ten-year-olds know about something like this? Still, I looked into Getouttahere's brown eyes and wondered what he really thought. He just wagged his tail and then licked my hand. I was tired of thinking about serious stuff, so we played fetch instead. I was good at throwing the ball and he was good at bringing it back, an equal partnership.

If dogs could talk it would take
a lot of the fun out of owning one.

Over the next couple of days, I thought
about that talk me and Papa had had. I
wasn't really thinking so much about the
God part of it but about what dogs must be
thinking. Papa said they didn't think. I
wasn't so sure, not that I didn't believe him.
A dog has a brain. It must be able to use part
of it for thinking.

Papa thought chickens were brainless. He'd
point out the stupid things they did to make
his argument valid. Chickens would eat
anything, and I do mean anything. Papa said
if chickens had a brain at all, why would
they watch him prepare one of their own for
the dinner table but not run from him the
next time he went inside the chicken pen.
They were stupid, that's why, he would say.

When his old mule wouldn't do what he told
it to do, he said he was being stubborn. Did
that mean mules could think? Isn't being
stubborn a thought? Papa sometimes called
Granny a stubborn old mule. Papa would
talk to that old mule, not Granny, but the
one that pulled the garden plow. Why would
he talk to something that couldn't think?
Sure, the mule couldn't talk back but that
didn't mean that he didn't understand every
single word Papa said.

I often sat around and talked to Getouttahere. We were best friends and best friends talked to one another. Well, in this case he seemed to at least be a good listener. He acted liked he cared about what I was saying. He would wag is tail, lick me or just cock his head one way or the other, flicking his one good ear. Maybe he used sign language. His facial expressions were priceless, if you can actually call them expressions.

It could just be my imagination getting the best of me again. I sometimes caught myself pretending he was answering me, wondering just how his talking voice might sound. On television they had Francis the talking mule and Mister Ed the Palomino that could talk to Wilbur, his owner. Why couldn't there be a talking dog? Just what might he say? My wild and wooly imagination launched into overdrive.

Tyler, that would be me, *why is it that I always have to be the one chasing and fetching that stupid red ball? We could take turns and you could go get it occasionally.* He sounded just like Mister Ed. What did I really know about dog voices? It would have to do, I suppose. At least he didn't call me Wilbur.

Dog food, I get it but why would you think the only thing I would prefer having is a bag lunch? I watch the rest of you eating pork chops and chicken. You don't so much as toss me a mere morsel. I do accept table scraps. And I do like in between meal snacks. Just keeping that bowl filled with the same old stuff isn't the way the rest of you do it. I thought I was part of the big happy family. Even a change of brands would be better than nothing. I might as well be chewing on your father's old leather loafers. At least I could pretend it was a rawhide bone. He might not quite see it that way though.

What's with this always opening the door and trying to get me to go outside? I'm cozy and comfy inside. Right, you call it, me going out there to do my business. None of you go outside to do your business; well, that Frankie kid sometimes does, and you do use the old man's outhouse when we're there. Why would you think I want to go out there to do mine? Your father tricks me all the time. He goes out and snookers me into following him. He then slips back inside and leaves me out there. It was funny the first hundred or so times. I'm not sure why I always fall for it. Maybe I just don't want to hurt his feelings. He seems so on edge most of the time. He really needs to learn to relax.

Your mother, I do like her, but she really should do something about that nighttime snoring. When she hits her stride, she can sound like a pack of snarling wolves. And what's with your grandpa always blaming his farts on me? All right, I confess, I'm not completely innocent but is it so wrong for him to sometimes take the blame?

How do you put up with that kid pal of yours? He's always putting you down and making up stuff. If ever I wanted to bite anyone, he's a prime candidate. He better be glad I'm not a biter. Besides, I would probably catch rabies from him if I did.

Tell that father of yours that I'm growing a bit tired of his talk about having me neutered. I came into this world with what I have, and I'd like to leave it with all of it still in tack.

Can you give me a little breathing room sometimes, how about it? This being joined at the hip and going everywhere together is getting a little old. Make some new friends. Cut me some slack. Sometimes even a dog requires a little alone time. And for the record, I don't chase cars. Tell that kid to stop filling your head with such nonsense. What would I do with a vehicle if I caught one?

*Can we lose the collar? It chaffs my neck.
I'm really not into accessorizing. Plus, I
know where I live. I could probably find my
way back before you could. Maybe you
should wear it instead. Your sense of
direction is pretty lousy. You're apt to get
lost before me.*

Enough, already, maybe you being able to
talk would just take the fun out of
everything. I would have to agree with one
thing though. What we do tends to be more
for us and not you, and it is much easier to
blame shameful things we do on you. You
could never be a snitch. Getouttahere
wagged his tail, a puddle of drool gathered
on the floor below his snout. He was just too
trustworthy but still a good listener. Leaving
the talking to mules and horses was
probably the best thing for everyone.

*Just play along. This is better than the last
gig I had. The boy isn't a half bad host.*

Anybody who doesn't know what soap tastes like never washed a dog.

There's really nothing worse than a stinky dog. Ask mama. I don't mean bad breath stinky but sometimes he could use a breath mint. Dogs, just like us kids, do get dirty. Papa says if you get out in the hot sun and exert yourself, expect to ooze ignorant oil. That's what he calls sweat, not just any ole sweat, but what he calls it when people don't know any better than to pick the worst time of the day to do something and get wet to their underwear. He says there is nothing at all wrong with sweating. It's healthy for you but getting sweaty when you didn't intend to do so is when you bleed ignorant oil. He says, don't dress for church and then decide to do a chore. Ignorant oil will be your just reward.

Getouttahere is usually clean and stink-free. I don't think he understands Papa's rules on sweating. I'm not even sure if dos sweat. Frankie told me that dogs sweat though their tongues. That's why they are always drooling. I had heard that even before Frankie pretended to be the expert. I planned to ask Papa but instead I asked Daddy first.

Daddy wasn't sure, so he asked a friend who was a friend of a veterinarian, not Getouttahere's doggy doctor. Daddy told me that dogs do drool to lower the heat in their body, but that their tongue was not really sweating. I couldn't wait to tell Frankie.

The veterinarian had passed along the word that most of a dog's sweat glands are located on the pads of its feet and on its nose. On a hot day he said you may notice a dog leaving behind a trail of wet footprints as it walks across a smooth, dry surface. That's dog sweat. Dogs sweat through their feet, how about that?

Mama complains about Daddy's sweaty feet all the time. She makes him leave his work boots on the porch. She calls it allowing them to air out because they smell bad. Mama is sort of the stink police at our house. She sniffs out everything. Daddy said she must be part bloodhound. That's just too funny.

Sometimes she tells me I need a bath. I used to think it was because I was dirty from head to toe, but maybe I stink too. I tried smelling myself once after she told me that, but I smelled like me to me. It is summer and after breakfast I can't wait to get outside. No shirt, no shoes, no problem, I do what Papa calls ripping and romping all day, wearing nothing but my cut-off jeans. Mama makes me come inside for lunch then I'm good to go until supper time. I'm back outside until dark thirty most days. My best friend is with me, two peas in a pod, just like Papa and me.

A cousin visited us last summer from New Jersey. He was two years older than me and talked really funny. He frowned when I said we could stay outside and play until dark thirty. Come to think of it, he frowned at a lot of things I said. I guess I frowned at a lot of things he said too. At first, I thought he was speaking a foreign language. Mama called it a Jersey accent.

Joey, that was his name, asked me about my accent. I told him I didn't have an accent. I sounded like this all the time and pointed out to him that he was the only one that sounded different. He didn't sound like anybody from around here and he talked way too fast.

Papa said Joey's daddy and uncles were wise guys. I guess that's what they call smart people from New Jersey. Joey called Getouttahere, just plain ole Outtahere. I corrected him for awhile until he told me to 'forgetaboutit'. All his words sort of run together. I think that's why he could talk so fast.

Frankie didn't like Joey. He never said why. I think it was because Joey liked to pick on Frankie. My Jersey cousin was a bully in some ways. He cursed too. If I said some of the things, he said I would be eating soap for a week. My new name would be Mister Bubbles if that happened.

The stink patrol had sniffed out my dog. During breakfast Mama told me to give Getouttahere a bath or he was staying outside. I gave her one of those, *but mama* responses and she gave me that look that told me that she meant every single word. I knew better than to argue with her. I had never given a dog a bath before, so I wasn't exactly sure how to pull this off.

Not to fear, my advisors, Frankie and Joey were more than willing to tell me how to make Getouttahere clean as a whistle. Frankie said we could just soak him with the hose pipe, which prompted Joey to ask, *what is a hose pipe*? Joey just wasn't up on southern words.

Frankie walked him to the backyard and just pointed. Joey got it, a garden hose. Frankie confirmed, *yep, a hose pipe*. Joey said he had washed his dog plenty of times in the bathtub. That wasn't going to work. The tub was inside the bathroom which was inside the house. Mama had said I couldn't bring my dog inside until I washed him first. Papa would call this putting the cart in front of the horse. I never understood that saying until this very moment.

Joey said we would have to improvise. Frankie asked him to speak English. We'd have to find a replacement for the bathtub, something outside explained my Jersey boy cousin. I got it. We'd have to make do. We had to find something we could fill with water, something big enough for Getouttahere to fit in.

We came up empty in my yard. Frankie snapped his fingers saying he had the perfect place. His little sister, Eva, had a brand-new inflatable paddle pool. Joey looked confused and mumbled something laced with curse words in Jersey talk. Frankie rolled his eyes and said swimming pool. Joey got it then and added we would need soap. Frankie said not to worry; there was plenty of soap stuff at his house just perfect for washing a dog. I had plenty of help and a place to give him a bath. How hard could it be?

We arrived at Frankie's house and we were in luck, the coast was clear. A note on the kitchen table indicated that Eva and their mother had gone to the grocery store. Frankie had snatched up a bottle of Ivory soap detergent. We were in luck. The hose pipe at their house was long enough to reach the paddle pool.

I pointed to the water and told Getouttahere to get in. He didn't and wouldn't. Frankie was squirting the contents of the Ivory bottle into the paddle pool. He saved half the bottle, Joey saying we would have to squirt the rest on my dog and lather him up.

So far, my dog was not wet or lathered or inside the pool. Joey just stood there holding the hose pipe while Frankie and I tried to boy-handle Getouttahere into the paddle pool. It's hard to make both ends of dog go to the same place at the same time. I had him around his neck and Frankie was pushing at his hinny. We had our hands full and were making no headway or tail way.

Joey dropped the hose pipe. He'd argue garden hose. He grabbed my dog's middle section. With shear brute boy force we wrestled the stinky dog inside the paddle pool. We pushed on his hinny to make him sit in the water. All three of us were in the now crowded pool with him. Joey sloshed water on him saying for us to do the same. We had to get him good and wet first. I think we were wetter than him.

So far, we managed to keep him in a sitting position. Joey began squirting him with the Ivory stuff, using the other half of the bottle. He was lathering up all right. We were too. Frankie and I held him tight while Joey got the hose and aimed it at him and unfortunately us. Soap suds were multiplying by the second. We looked like a bunch of deformed snowmen and one snow dog. It was way too slippery too. We took times falling. Somehow, we managed to keep a hold on Getouttahere.

I glanced over at Frankie and he looked like a dog with rabies, foaming at the mouth and all. It was about then that I got my first good taste of the Ivory soap. It didn't taste anything like the snow now piling up and out of the pool. I knew that very moment that I'd never ever cursed in front of my parents or anyone who would wash my mouth out with soap.

The paddle pool had flooded over and now the yard was taking on the likeness of an avalanche. Joey had dropped the hose pipe and was now trying to help us keep my dog in the pool. He was covered head to toe now too and even had a long white sudsy beard. We were all laughing up a storm. The only one who didn't think it was funny was Getouttahere. He was still squirming and shaking off suds.

The screen door slamming shut tipped us off that we had been busted. There stood Frankie's mother and his little sister. Her face had that same look I had seen way too many times on Mama's face. Eva was mimicking her and striking the same pose. We were in for it now. Frozen in our sudsy snowmen suits, we dropped our guard.

Getouttahere bolted, leaving a white bubbly trail behind him. Me and Joey waved as we back peddled and then made a hasty retreat. If we were lucky, she wouldn't be able to recognize us. My wishful imagination wasn't going to save us this time.

Later Joey just made matters worse. He tried to make it sound like it was my Mama's fault, saying she was the one who made me give him a bath. He had just been trying to help. He threw Frankie under the bus playing up the fact it had been his idea to use the pool and the bottle of liquid soap.

Mama cringed when she realized we had used the entire bottle of dish water detergent. She phoned Frankie's mom saying she would replace it. Getouttahere was not allowed in the house that night and I was in the doghouse along with him. Somehow, I had lucked out and hadn't been given a whipping by Daddy. I hated going into the yard and picking my very own switch. Joey didn't get that one either. I just ignored his questions this time.

A door is what a dog is perpetually on the wrong side of.

After Papa had originally convinced everyone that I should get a shot at having a dog as a pet, the decision had to be made if Getouttahere would be considered as being an inside or an outside dog. I didn't realize so many decisions were important. Papa pondered on it. Papa was good at pondering. I hadn't quite grasped the art of pondering yet. Papa told me it would come in due time. He rubbed his chin and looked at my dog from head to tail, finally saying Getouttahere might be an *inbetweener*.

In between what, I asked him. Midsized dogs could go either way he replied. He leaned towards judging him to be an outside dog. I was afraid he would wander back off to where he came from if he stayed outside. Papa sort of agreed, changing his mind and conceding that it might be best that he stayed inside with me to get used to his new surroundings and home. That's why Papa is so smart. I was relieved. Mama and Daddy went along with his suggestion on a trial basis. Daddy gave me a stern warning though; the dog was my responsibility and if things didn't work out, out would be the key word, outside he would go. I had never been under so much pressure before now. Being responsible didn't sound like it was going to be too easy or much fun.

Papa told me that I would have to first house break Getouttahere. Why would I want to own a broken dog? He smiled that big ole warm smile he gives me that makes me feel good inside. He then explained that dogs, like people, must do their business.
The quickest way for my dog to be kicked outside would be if he did his business inside the house.

House breaking meant training him to go outside when he needed to go to the bathroom. I had never thought about that. Having a pet was not going to be a piece of cake. Nothing worth wanting comes easy. Papa said training a puppy, while difficult, might still be easier than training an adult stray, already set in its ways and not accustomed to being hemmed up inside. Who was going to train me how to train Getouttahere?

I was out on one of those limbs, so Papa would often say. My only resource was Frankie and he always wanted to help, but he too often guessed at things. Guessing and not being lucky can get you in a whole heap of trouble. Frankie stayed in trouble, so it seemed. Too often I got caught up in his, a victim by association is what Daddy called it.

Papa gave me a few pointers, but it was still left up to me to make sure accidents didn't happen in the house. Frankie said that if he did poop on or wet the floor for me to make sure I cleaned it up before my parents knew that it had happened. My pal didn't volunteer to help though. He was an idea man, not always a doer.

Whew…my brain was having a tough time keeping all this stuff straight. I didn't want to be the one to mess it up and be the cause of my dog staying outside. Well, he might not think it was all that bad because he had lived outside from the best any of us could tell. Would he even like living inside a house? I sure liked staying outside, playing for as long as I could, with dark thirty forcing me inside most days.

Having a dog as a best friend had certainly altered my summer vacation plans. Responsibility was a big word with even bigger consequences if you got it wrong. Papa said that, not me. Consequences were a big word too. Both spelled trouble with a capital T.

Papa said for me to let him do his business outside before I took him inside. I sat on the

steps watching him sit there watching me.
Go do your business I told him, but he just
waged his tail and lapped his tongue at me.
This wasn't exactly working.

After a long time passed, and a long time is
really a long time in a kid's mind, I decided
to do something different. I walked around
in the yard. Getouttahere followed me.
When I stopped, he stopped. When I walked,
he walked. Business wasn't getting done.
Being held responsible for him doing his
business wasn't exactly fun either. Maybe
he just didn't have to go. One thing for sure,
my new friend, for whatever reason, wasn't
leaving my side. He could have just run off,
never to be seen again, but he didn't. A dog
that Papa had tried to run off didn't want to
go anywhere or do anything.

It was time to try something different. I told
Getouttahere to come on, follow me, and we
went inside. I sure hoped he didn't change
his mind now that we were no longer
outside. I refilled his food bowl and
freshened up his water dish. He watched me
but didn't eat or drink from either one of
them. We went to my room to wait some
more.

There, I looked at him. He looked back at
me. It was almost like having a stare off. Me
and Frankie have stare offs all the time,

seeing who will laugh or blink first. Dogs don't laugh and I think he blinks a lot less than me, no contest there. Bored, I began playing with match box cars. He flopped down on the floor but kept watching me. Soon he was on his side sound asleep. My eyes were getting heavy too. It is hard work waiting. A wet tongue on my face woke me up.

He half barked and half whined at me. I patted him on the head and he then did it again. He did it a third time even louder and was almost backing away from me as if to get me to follow him. He had food and water so what was his problem. I wiped the sleep from my eyes and stood. He went into the hallway and then came back and woofed at me again. I guess we were playing follow the leader and I must be the follower. We ended up in the den near the sliding glass door. He scratched on the door, turned and woofed at me. I got it. He wanted to go outside.

I opened the door and he shot like a streak through it. I kept on following him. To my surprise, he found a spot he liked in the backyard and did his business there. Getouttahere had just trained me to take him outside. He was house broken. He was either real smart or it meant this was not his first time inside a house. Not the first time inside, now that worried me. It worried me a lot. Could that mean that my dog had run away from home? Maybe a kid like me was missing his dog.

Before I had time to ponder, and I didn't realize I was, Getouttahere woofed and ran down the hallway again. He stood at the sliding glass back door. I got it. He wanted to go outside. I was getting the hang of this doing his business thing. I let him out and followed. This time he just stood there on the porch and looked at me. We were outside, now what? What was he training me to do this time? He wagged his tail and then just sat down.

A lifetime passed so it seemed. I decided to open the door. Without warning, he raced past me and headed to his food dish. He gobbled down half of it and then lapped some water. I called for him to follow me to my room. He did. A few minutes later he woofed at me and down the hallway he went. He wanted to go outside again, so I opened the door. He dashed out and then just sat there. It seemed my new dog had monkey business in mind instead.

We did the inside, outside thing over and over, no business being done on either side of that door. Mama had seen some of it and told me to either stay in or out. I was letting flies in the house she warned. Tell my dog how about it, I wanted to say but didn't. I took Getouttahere back to my room and closed my bedroom door. That should fix things. Should, but it didn't. Now not only did he woof at me, he began scratching at my bedroom door and I mean really scratching it. He was leaving claw marks, not good for him or me. I'd grab him by the collar and pulled him away.

As soon as I would turn him loose, he would be back at it again. There was nothing to do now but go back outside. This time he did his business. I felt really bad that I hadn't listened to him. We did the in and out thing a few more times, no business being done. I'm not sure if he cried uncle or me first, but finally he stopped and curled up at the foot of my bed. Papa would later tell me that the bad thing about having an inside dog is that they are always on the wrong side of the door. I didn't have to ponder that one.

If your dog is fat
you're not getting enough exercise.

I'm pretty skinny. Some might say way too skinny, but I'm a kid. I rip and I romp and I'm not one to just sit around and do nothing. Sure, I love eating junk food, just like any other kid and never pass up a chance to feed my sweet tooth, as Papa calls it. Having a dog for a pet gives even me a run for my money. He likes to rip and romp too.

Papa usually calls most dogs, good for nothing, flea bitten and mangy, and just plain fat and lazy. I haven't heard him call Getouttahere any of those names so far. Maybe my dog is growing on him or maybe he just doesn't say those things because he is my dog. One thing for sure, he's not flea bitten or mangy. I'm not sure exactly what mangy means but I don't think he is just the same. He's certainly not fat or lazy. I'm not sure yet if he's good for nothing. He's definitely good at going outside and back inside. I'm not sure if Papa would count that one though.

I have seen fat dogs. My Aunt Glenda has a real fat dog. It wobbles when it walks, and I've never seen it run. It's one of those bulldogs, the kind you see on cartoons, droopy jaws, short legged, belly nearly dragging the ground and always drooling from its tongue. I'm glad my dog isn't that breed of dog. I would have to mop up behind it all the time or it would become an outside dog in a flash.

Papa says you could judge a dog by its owner. He says after a while they start to look alike. Does that mean I'm going to grow spots and look like mine? I thought about what he had said the next time I was visiting my aunt with the fat bulldog. I was shocked. She was fat and had droopy jaws too. I never saw Aunt Glenda drool and she does keep her tongue in her mouth, but she is slow moving like Clyde, her dog.

Papa claims that if you're fat, your dog is going to be fat too. Most dogs, except for Clyde, enjoy exercise. I don't mean doing push-ups and sit-ups or stuff like that. Dogs like to run and play, just like kids do. People in our neighborhood are forever taking their dogs for a walk. *Walking the Dog* is a song. Rufus Thomas sang the song. I have the album. Now that I think of it, it had a picture of Rufus and a bulldog on it. I can also walk the dog with my yo-yo, but not that good though. Frankie can do all sorts of yo-yo tricks with his red Imperial Duncan yo-yo.

I knew a girl at school who named her weenie dog, *Yo-Yo*. I thought that was a stupid name for a dog at the time. She would probably think the same about Getouttahere. She didn't look like a weenie dog though, not that I can remember. I don't pay that much attention to girls, so I could be wrong.

I sort of started paying attention to people and their dogs. Did fat people have fat dogs and were skinny dogs always with skinny people? I was beginning to think that maybe Papa was yanking my chain. He always says there is nothing wrong with a little harmless fun. He warned me to never be hurtful and mean when funning a friend or stranger. Never call people names and never bully other kids. I was too skinny and scrawny to call other kids names or bully them. Plus, I wasn't stupid either.

One good thing about having a dog for a pet, at least a large one, is that other kids don't tend to pick on you as much; especially if you threaten to sic your dog on them. Saying you have an attack dog is an attention getter. Innocent fibs never hurt, especially if you never get caught at it.

Aunt Glenda's Clyde sure looked the part with those big teeth poking from its mouth. Sadly, ole Clyde would probably drop dead of a heart attack if he tried to attack anyone.

He'd come closer to slobbering someone to death; death by drowning in dog drool...yuck!

Tina down the street has two cats as pets. People must not look like cats. She didn't look like either one of hers. She was fat though. The cats weren't. I should probably ask Papa about that the next time I visit my grandparents or when they come over to our house. I was going to make sure I didn't get judged by how my dog looked unless it was something good said. Right now, Getouttahere didn't have the slightest smidgen of fat and that's the way I intended to keep it. I didn't want people to point at the fat dog and his fat owner.

Thinking back, maybe I should have done better with my goldfish. How do you walk a fish, though? I dropped the thought as quickly as I thought about it. I sure couldn't allow Frankie to catch wind of this sort of thinking. I'd never hear the end of it.

Just going in and out that sliding door like we do all the time should give us both plenty of exercise and keep us fat free. Throwing balls and fetching sticks can wear you out too after awhile, and I'm not even the one chasing them. Weebles wobble but they don't fall down. I'm not sure why I thought that, except, Weebles were sort of fat on the bottom and a Yo-yo wobbled, not that either one of these things has anything to do with the other. I think about stuff all the time but a lot of it doesn't always make much sense. That's why I keep it inside my head and don't let it escape my mouth. *Fatty, fatty, two by four, can't get through the kitchen door* is a mean tune kids sing and taunt fat kids with. I never have, but I've heard Frankie do it. I wasn't about to give anyone the chance to sing that about me and Getouttahere.

Kids can be so cruel and like name calling others. I should know. I've been called skinny-weenie, skeleton and toothpick, but not since I've gotten my attack dog. One little sick um works wonders on the bullies. *Your dog is fat, you're not getting enough exercise, Tyler.* I promise you; nobody is ever going to say that about me or Getouttahere. We're going to look alike in a good way if I have anything to do with it.

**I wonder what goes through his mind
when he sees us peeing in his water bowl.**

Having a dog for a pet can gross you out. I
don't gross out easily. I'm usually good at
doing things to gross out girls. I'm as good
at grossing out girls as Papa is pondering
about stuff. Papa says everybody must be
good at something. If you're not, you're not
trying hard enough.

Getouttahere might have taken over my king
of the hill gross out title. That dog will eat
about anything and I do mean anything.
You'd think he was some sort of wild wolf
or something. Papa says all dogs came from
wolves. Somewhere in the back of their
minds they think they still are. He calls it
primal instinct. That's why dogs will catch
and kill things. Papa says there is nothing
worse than a dog that kills chickens. You
can't break them from doing it once they
have started. He says there is only one cure;
shoot them. I'm keeping mine clear of any
of his chickens.

That doesn't stop him from sniffing, licking
and eating stuff, stuff I can't even identify.
Maybe living on his own taught him to eat
anything when he could find it. I'm still not
so sure he lived too long by himself. After
all, he was already house broken. You can't
learn that from being outside all the time.

Papa says there is a lot we don't know about him. We didn't raise him from a puppy and really don't know exactly how old he is. It's like starting in the middle of something and just guessing at it. The fact he didn't run away when Papa tried to chase him off means he likes people. Papa says that probably means he has never been mistreated by any. If he had been, he wouldn't so openly trust people. *Never bite the hand that feeds you* is one of Papa's favorite sayings.

I'm still not sure why I have to spend so much time making sure Getouttahere's dishes are kept clean and he has fresh water. He'll certainly lap water up most anywhere. I've seen him drink water out of the dirtiest and nastiest mud puddles. I've even seen him licking up water off the driveway while Daddy is washing the car. I'm always surprised he's not foaming at the mouth from the soapsuds. None of it ever seems to make him sick.

Frankie and I were playing down by the creek late one summer afternoon, a real scorcher Papa calls them, and we decided to drink the flowing creek water. It looked clean enough. It tasted good and cold. Getouttahere lapped up his fair share too. Frankie and I ended up with the squirts, unable to stray too far from the bathroom.

Getouttahere was fine and he probably drank more than both of us combined. Papa told us that a dog has a strong constitution. I thought for once he must be making that up; what did a dog know about The Constitution? I'm a kid and barely knew.

One of his favorite places to drink water was from the toilet. There was nothing that made Mama madder than to catch him lapping up water from the toilet bowl. She would purposely go around and close the toilet lids. In the middle of the night, half asleep, I have made a mess on the floor because the lid was down. She fussed at me about that too. For a little while I was fearful, she might make me go outside.

Papa says to dogs, water is water. They don't know the difference between right and wrong places to drink. Most animals aren't picky when they are thirsty. People are though, unless they're stranded in the middle of the desert or some wilderness. Drinking or dying from thirst tends to change your mind, even if it gives you the squirts later. I guess it made sense. I just hope I never get lost or stranded.

I wondered what Getouttahere might be thinking. After all, he had watched me pee many times in the toilet. Did he think I was peeing in his personal water dish? If he did, it didn't seem to stop him. Maybe he thought the flush got rid of all the bad water and replaced it with clean water. I guess that was sort of true. That's why we flushed afterwards.

But if clean water was what we now had, why was it that Mama was always constantly cleaning the toilet bowl. Did she think someday we might have to drink from the toilet bowl to survive one of those 'end of the world' battles? Now I was scaring myself. There's no sense in me trying to outthink my dog. He's going to do what he wants to do. If drinking nasty water from anywhere and everywhere is it, then that's just the way it is.

I wonder if other dogs think poodles are members of a weird religious cult.

I didn't give it much thought when I laid claim to Getouttahere, but there are a lot of different kinds of dogs. Daddy said he read some place that there were over 300 different dog breeds. The way Papa tells it, my dog must be a mix of a bunch of them. He said Getouttahere may as soon be one as another. I asked him to please stop calling my dog a sooner. He did, but that doesn't make him stop thinking it though. I'm glad dogs don't bully other dogs who are different. Kids could learn a lot from dogs if they just paid some attention.

Well, I reckon I would ignore that butt smelling thing they do. It can be embarrassing when you run into someone else who has a dog and the first thing your dog wants to do is take a sniff. Papa told me not to worry about it. It is what dogs do. Cats don't do that, why do dogs do it? Sometimes when I try to make Getouttahere stop, both dogs get riled at one another. Papa keeps telling me, *son, just let it run its course; it's not hurting a thing.*

Asking why things are the way they are, is a kid's rite of passage. We're going to do it and grown-ups expect that we are going to do it. It's an unwritten law or something like that. No one should be surprised, frustrated or disappointed when it happens. Naturally, I wasn't going to just let this butt sniffing thing go. I latched onto it like a hungry dog on a bone, so Papa likes to say.

Why do dogs act this way around other dogs? Like I've said, Papa always has an answer for everything. He explained that a dog has a powerful sense of smell, a lot better than plain ole people. He likened the smelling exercise to people greeting each other with a friendly handshake. I'm glad we shake hands. He said that dogs find out a lot about the other dog by taking that whiff. Every dog smells different. I asked papa what sort of things they found out, but he wrinkled up his nose, like he had smelled a fart or something.

He took a big ole breath, placed his hand on my shoulder and told me dogs can tell if the other dog is a boy or girl dog, and if it is a 'she', does she want a boyfriend. He said they can tell what the other dog has eaten recently. That sort of makes sense. Is the dog a friend or a foe? Even if the dogs are friends, they still sniff every time they meet, that hand shaking thing again. When somebody owns more than one dog and they get all worked up and stressed out, they'll do this smelling thing too, to calm one another down.

Papa looked me in the eyes and finally said, "I hope that's enough to satisfy your curiosity." That was Papa's way of saying he was done talking about the subject. I nodded. I was done too. Stick a fork in me is what Papa usually says.

I kept paying attention to other dogs when I saw them, and not to see if they did the sniffing thing, but more to see how each was different from the next. I hadn't really done that before having my own dog. A dog had just been a dog; some bigger or smaller, friendlier or meaner than the next one, but just dogs.

I since have figured out that dogs are really a lot like people in their looks. No, people don't look like dogs and dogs don't look like people, but all are sort of different, even when they are the same breed of dog. One thing for sure, I hadn't seen any that looked like mine. As bad as I hate to say it, I reckon papa was right about his sooner talk, even though I sooner not want to think about it. Some say people grow to look like their dogs. If true, I'm not sure who I should pity in some cases, the dog or the person.

Papa says it is hard to beat having a good hunting dog. Looks don't mean squat to hear him tell it, provided the dog can chase rabbits, point out birds or retrieve downed waterfowl. He's just not into one as a pet. He's still not fooling me though. I know he likes Getouttahere.

Many kinds of dogs do look funny. The weenie dog, dash hound, Dachshund or whatever you want to call those long, short legged critters, are mighty odd looking. My cousin has two. One is named Oscar and the other, Frank. One of my friends has a sheepdog but he doesn't have any sheep. I don't know how that dog can see where it is going with hair blocking its view.

Rachel from up the street has a miniature hairless rat looking dog, ugly with a capitol *U*. I wonder if dogs think about what other dogs look like or are they just interested in butt sniffing.

What I don't get is why some people give their dog's haircuts. If the dog was supposed to look different, they would be different. Dogs have certain types of hair just like they come in small, big and extra large. It seems all wrong to me to shape them up differently.

My aunt has a French Poodle, but it isn't from France. Go figure. The dog has long, pretty white hair, but my aunt doesn't like long, pretty hair for some reason. She has the dog all chopped up with white fur balls on its legs, the back half of it shaved, and the front part still puffy and shaped. She even puts big red bows on its ears. It looks like a fake dog to me.

I wonder how Getouttahere sees it. Might he look at this odd creature and wonder what religion or cult it belongs to, or if it has been in some sort of weed whacker accident. I wonder if butt scent revealed any strange oddities about such a handcrafted critter. I would be ashamed to go out in public if someone trimmed me up like that.

Poodle, even the name sounds weird for a dog. Maybe she should call him Doodle the Poodle or even Yankee Poodle. I should be ashamed of myself for making up stuff like that, but I must admit, seeing that disjointed snowball just brings out the worse in me.

Getouttahere might see nothing wrong with the powder puff. I'll have to pay close attention if they cross one another's path and observe just how the butt sniffing goes. A dog might just be a dog to another dog, no matter how it looks to people. I'm glad my stray didn't end up being a poodle. I don't know if Papa would have been willing to help me convince my folks to let me keep a poodle. I would have just let its hair grow back and not have trimmed it. I'm glad I have Getouttahere. What you see is what you get with him, no frills, no bows and no haircut. That's about all I have to say about it.

I am not your dog, but if every time you saw me, you gave me a backrub, I would run to greet you, too.

Why is it that Getouttahere loves getting his back rubbed? He'll freeze dead in his tracks if I begin rubbing or scratching him. Sometimes he'll even join. His hindfoot will break into a fidgety scratching fury. It's funny to watch him curl up his snout and eye me over his shoulder. Maybe his back is the one place he can't reach. I wonder if fleas know that the center of his back is a safety zone.

Getouttahere in general seems to scratch a lot without my help. I wonder if dogs are born with an itch. Mama sometimes rubs my back. I must confess. It does feel good. Sometimes she even scratches my back, even when it isn't itching. It feels just as good without the itch, maybe even better.

Sometimes when I'm rubbing or scratching Getouttahere, he just starts scratching with his paw in mid air. I stop, he stops. I start back and so does he. It's just too funny. Papa says dogs are just lazy by nature and rubbing them just makes them that much lazier. I've never seen Papa rub or scratch any dog. Dogs are not his best friends. Just ask him. He'll tell you exactly what he thinks.

Papa claims to be what he calls a straight shooter. For a long time, I just thought that meant he was good shot. He does his fair share of hunting, so why wouldn't I think that. Mama says Papa tells it like it is and can have strong opinions about most everything. She says he too often speaks his mind. I've seen Papa scratch his itch and sometimes it can be in some of the funniest places. Mama warned me that she better not catch me scratching myself there while in public, no matter how badly I itched.

Cats don't seem to scratch like dogs do, not as much any hoot. Most of the cats I've been around, tend to lick themselves silly. Dogs lick too. Mama would be the first to tell me not to copy their bad habits. Don't let mama fool you. She likes having her back rubbed just like the next person. Daddy buys her gift certificates for her birthday. She goes to some fancy place where people are paid to rub her back. Back rubs are free.

Why would anybody want to pay to get one? I could charge Getouttahere but how would he pay me if I did? Dogs don't have money. Maybe Lassie has his very own money because he is TV and movie star? I've never seen anyone rub his back and Lassie start scratching. Maybe it's not allowed on television or in a movie.

Rubbing, scratching, patting, Getouttahere is proud to be on the receiving end of any of them. I wonder if that is why he is happy to see me. He's looking forward to me rubbing his back. I reckon I would act the same way if I knew I was about to receive a backrub. Most people just shake hands when they greet one another. I've never seen them walk toward the other person backwards, expecting that person to rub their back.

Maybe I'll try it and see if Mama gets it. Forget trying it on Papa. He would just ask what was wrong with me, probably feel my head to see if I was running a temperature and then make me go back home and climb in bed until I felt better. It's not smart to play jokes on him. It's best to be one of those straight shooters.

I wish every time Mama saw me, she would rub my back. What's that old saying; I'll scratch your back if you scratch mine. It's like making a square deal with somebody. I might even come inside early for a back-rubbing reward, instead of kicking and screaming after dark thirty's arrival. You probably are wondering, so I'll just go ahead and tell you. Dark thirty is that time just before dark. In the summer it's no big deal because it stays daylight real late. In the wintertime though, dark thirty is my worst enemy. It gets dark way too soon. It seems

like not long after I get home from school it
is already nighttime.

Night or day, winter or summer,
Getouttahere is always up for a back rub. I
think he expects one, like I owe it to him or
something. Papa says I have that mangy
mutt spoiled rotten. It's possible. I know one
thing for sure though. If every time you saw
me, you gave me a backrub, I would run to
greet you too, and I'm not a dog. And I still
don't think my dog is mangy, whatever
mangy is supposed to mean.

There is a reason a Dog
has so many friends.

Papa kept calling Getouttahere a sooner
even though he knew I didn't like him
saying that. I don't think he can help himself
or that's what granny says. She says you
can't change the colors of an old coot that is
set in his ways. She said she stopped trying
many years ago. I don't think he really
means to be hurtful. He just doesn't like four
legged varmints in general, freeloaders so he
sees them. My dog doesn't appear to take
offense.

I guess it's because Papa doesn't say it in a
mean tone. Mama says Papa has this unique
way of speaking his mind, and then you
have to sit back and think about it before
you realize what he just said wasn't meant to
be nice. By then it's too late. He's either
moved onto a new subject or has left all
together. Some people give Papa what they
call a pass because he's an elder. I wish they
would give me a pass sometimes. I guess
when I'm old like him they might. Kids get
no such breaks.

Frankie, my best friend forever, likes my
dog, thank goodness. Frankie can look at
things differently from anybody else I know.
He says he thinks about important stuff.
There are thinkers and then there are doers,

so he says. Frankie brags that he is both, all rolled into one neat little package. I've never seen anyone who could look at the very same thing I'm looking at but then spin it differently. Frankie, the thinker and doer, can.

Sometimes his thinking causes us do stuff that gets us into trouble. When that happens, Frankie just shrugs it off and admits he just over-thunk it. He thinks *thunk* is a word and I can't convince him otherwise. Frankie has a certain way of talking and tosses in his very own words and phrases, but that's just Frankie being Frankie.

Take tail wagging for an example. Frankie has come up with what he calls a theory on dogs wagging their tails. He has a theory for most everything. I think he makes most of it up, but you'll never win an argument to convince him otherwise. Come to think of it, I'm not sure I have ever won an argument with Frankie. I usually just cry uncle and am done with it. Most of it isn't that important anyway; well, only to Frankie. He claims tail wags sooth humans. It's that thump, thump, thump back and forth that kind of hypnotizes people; well, maybe all except Papa. He says most people suffer from low self esteem and like to be liked. Dogs wagging their tails do just that.

I wasn't sure if Frankie made up that *low self-esteem* part, but he claimed these words were in the dictionary. I checked and they were and sort of matched what he was explaining. I just boosted his already big old fat ego head by doing that.

Frankie didn't just stop at that. He never just stops at a short point to be made. There's always more; sometimes endless babble. I think he just likes to hear himself talk. He went on by saying people are gravitated to dogs and their tail wagging because it's better than listening to people wag their tongues. Frankie loves using words like *gravitated.* He added that people grow tired of other people talking so much. I couldn't argue with that one. The proof was right there in front of me. I didn't tell Frankie though, not that it would have hurt his feelings; it would have just given him another reason to go on and on.

Frankie doesn't need to be encouraged to do that. When I pat or rub my dog or talk to him and he wags his tail, I must admit, it does sooth me. He does wag his tongue too, both ends working at the same time. That's okay by me.

I thought we were done with the theorizing. What was I possibly thinking? This is Frankie. Ask him the time and he will tell you how to make a watch and then how to sell it and make a fortune. He doesn't know how to answer yes or no or use a simple shrug. I may as well sit back and take my medicine and let him get to a final ending. Interrupting him just makes it last longer. Luckily, we had no place to be. Well, lucky for him, maybe not me.

Dogs laugh with their tails. Frankie said that you could tell a lot about any dog by the way their tail was behaving. A quick wag meant the dog was happy, glad to see you, was probably greeting you with open paws. Frankie said that, not me. A slow wag meant the dog wasn't so sure, might not recognize you or might just plain not trust you or even dislike you. This was of course more Frankie theories. I asked him what if the dog doesn't wag its tail. It's tough to stump the answer man.

Frankie repeated exactly what I had just asked. I think he does this to stall for time until he can make up an answer. That's just my theory. There are two reasons he said that dogs don't wag their tales. Nothing was ever simple when Frankie was involved. Reason number one: The dog doesn't know you. He had to go there, that butt sniffing thing that dogs do to meet and greet one another. It sort of made sense though, that a dog wouldn't wag a tail at a stranger.

Frankie said a slow wag was almost as bad as a no wag. He said it meant that the dog wasn't sure if he liked or trusted you. Reason number two: The dog didn't like you and was gearing up to snap at you next. Frankie said you should offer the dog the back of your hand to sniff, a substitute for the butt, I reckon. Why would I offer up my hand to a dog that was probably going to bite me? Only a complete moron would do that. Surely this wasn't Frankie's way of saying I was a complete moron. He just smiled when I called him on it and then gave me a shrug. Now he finally decides to shrug.

Frankie's spins never end. He outdid himself this time. He said dogs were really people with short legs and fur coats. He said it was scientific fact. I told him he was full of it. Frankie absolutely never back petals when you call his bluff. He just digs the hole deeper and somehow has the knack of convincing you that he's about to strike it rich and discover gold or diamonds. He can do all this with a straight face. It's what Papa calls a poker face. He claims that dogs are reincarnated people. There he goes using those big words again.

Simply put, so says Frankie and Frankie never simply puts anything; people die and come back as dogs in another life. He watches way too many science fiction movies and believes what happens on them is real. I must admit now he had me wondering who had Getouttahere been before he became a dog. Frankie had managed to sucker me in again and I had never seen it coming. He was good at that too.

Okay, my turn, so I gave Frankie something to think about. I can do theory too if I set my mind to it. I tried to sound adult like in my logic to him. I cleared my throat, poked out my chest and without cracking so much as a smile I spoke my peace on the matter. I told him in my most serious voice, the more I see of man, the more I like dogs. My goal in life is to be as good of a person as Getouttahere already thinks I am. He giggled at my attempt at theory. I still didn't crack a smile and told him that if I came back as a dog, I wanted to be the same breed as Getouttahere.

He agreed with me but then he snuffed it out all in one breath. He told me that it was fitting that I come back as a mixed-up dog breed and that I better get that tail wagging part down pat if I expected to make friends in my afterlife. People don't particularly warm up to sooners. He even used Papa as an example. I hate it when Frankie puts up a good argument. I wagged my butt just to irritate him. He punched me in the arm. I pretended to snap at him. He then thumped me in the nose and called me a bad dog. Getouttahere just watched us like he thought we were both crazy. I can't blame him. I patted my best friend on the head, and he wagged his tail, no, not Frankie, my other best friend.

A cat, after being scolded, goes about its business. A dog slinks off into a corner and pretends to be doing a serious self-reappraisal.

Papa says a dog needs to always know its place. I thought his place was by my side, but Papa told me not to confuse matters. Sometimes Papa just plain confuses me with his facts and wisdom. He thinks I'm supposed to understand everything he says. I'm just a kid. I have a lot to learn yet, or so I've been told countless times by adults. I tend to be caught somewhere between I should know better and when I get older, I'll understand. I'm not so sure older is better but what do I know. I'm still learning theory and pondering. At least Getouttahere treats me the same no matter what I do or say.

Dogs must learn to mine and if they mess up, they need to be taught not to mess up again. It seems to me that kids must rate about the same as dogs. We always get put in our place for stuff we did or might be thinking about doing. How does a dog know the rules though, that fine line between right and wrong, royally messed up and in hot water? I don't think Getouttahere could pick his own switch from a bush. If he could I don't know if I can switch his legs with it. He has two more than me. Frankie claims that picking a switch is just a scare tactic to make us think about what we did and put the fear into us. Switches are real. I've had my legs and behind on the receiving end of one of those tree limbs.

Daddy's hand and belt are just as bad. Papa told me once after I received a spanking that parents sometimes have to whip their kids just to show them that they love them. I told Frankie that and he said that his parents must really love him.

Getouttahere has never done anything so bad that I wanted to whip him. That doesn't mean that I don't love him. He sometimes knocks over his water dish but so what, I spill lots of things. Accidents happen. His wanting to go out then back in is no call for me to spank him. He barks in the middle of the night and that really makes Daddy mad. Maybe that counts as one of those times he needs to know his place. I tell him to hush and he does, most of the time.

Daddy might see things differently. Getouttahere loves to dig dirt and his favorite place to dig is in Mama's flowerbed. That doesn't exactly make Mama cut cartwheels. Papa tells her the dog is digging for worms so we can go fishing. Mama has that look on her face that says she's doesn't appreciate Papa's explanations. Papa always reminds her that he is her daddy and for to hold her civil tongue. I'm not sure what kind of tongue Papa thinks she has.

Aunt Sarah, Papa's sister, has a lot of cats. We spent the day over at her house yesterday, so I thought I'd watch and hopefully see what happens if she must scold them. Scolding is not fun when you're the one being scolded. I wasn't sure if I was cut out for being the one that dished out a scolding. Getouttahere might stop liking me if I scolded him. Most of the day passed but no cat scolding happened. It looked like I wasn't going to learn much from the visit. At least it gave me something to do even if it turned out being nothing to do.

I finally hit pay dirt as Papa calls it. A calico cat jumped up on the kitchen table where Mama and Aunt Sarah were canning fig preserves. Boy how I hate figs preserved or in any fashion. Cooking them and putting them in jars seems to be a good place to keep them if you ask me. No one ever asked me though. Grape jelly, now I wish they would learn to preserve it. Anyway, that calico cat on the table riled both, Mama more fit to be tied than Aunt Sarah.

Aunt Sarah told the cat to scat. It didn't. Instead it sniffed one of the jars. Jar sniffing cats on a kitchen table brought out that look on Mama's face. I guess the cat had never seen her look before because it stayed on the table, sitting right there in the middle and started licking its paw. That did it, last straw, the one that is supposed to break a camel's back. I still don't get that saying.

Aunt Sarah slapped her hand down on that table making a thunderous sound. That calico scatted then, knocking two fig jars onto the floor, preserved figs and glass going everywhere. Scolding works better when you add a little more to it than just fussing, so it seems. The calico didn't stay gone very long though. A few minutes later it was right back in the kitchen, doing what Papa would call going about its business, paying nobody any attention. It was like the scolding had never happened.

The kitchen would have been the last place I would have wanted to be if it had happened to me. Cats after being scolded just go about their business as if it never happened or at least the calico had. Studying up on this was just making it more confusing for me. I needed to watch someone with dogs to help me decide what to do.

My cousin Pete has the two weenie dogs, Oscar and Frank. He just lives a couple of blocks from me. Tomorrow I would visit him and ask him how he does it; that is if he ever scolds Oscar and Frank. Why was scolding so important anyway? Maybe all dogs didn't need to be put in their place as Papa called it. He had yelled at Getouttahere the first time we had ever seen him, and he had slapped at his side to make him get and he hadn't. My dog might be perfect. Not according to Mama, Daddy and Papa though. Digging in the flower bed, always wanting to come in when he's outside and wanting to go out when he's inside didn't make the grownups very happy. Still, that didn't make him a bad dog, not in my book.

A visit to Cousin Pete's home did nothing to clear up the muddy water for me. He did have and did demonstrate his scolding technique, but we had to wait most of the day for Oscar or Frank to do something worthy of a scolding. Aunt Bessie arrived and from all the barking and ruckus neither of the weenie dogs seemed to like her very much. Pete clapped his hands loudly and shouted 'no' several times, but the two dogs didn't stop. A matter of a fact they sort of nipped at Aunt Bessie's ankles. Pete grabbed a fly swatter off a table and swatted each of the pups in their behinds. Tails tucked, the weenie dogs ran behind a huge chair in the corner of the room.

Pete called it slinking and said they'd stay there for a while until they thought no more swatting waited for them or until Aunt Bessie left. I watched the chair and the corner. Oscar and Frank would take turns peeking from behind the chair but they stayed put. I wasn't sure what I had just learned. I suppose dogs don't always mind the first time and fly swatters get their attention when they don't. Fly swatters are for flies, not dogs, and I would not be using one on Getouttahere. I'd find my own way if scolding ever became necessary.

**If you think dogs can't count
try putting three dog biscuits in your
pocket and then giving him
only two of them.**

My pals Bucky Bartholomew Owens and his
Cousin Elvis Aaaron Priestly dropped by my
house one afternoon having heard I now had
a dog. They used to be Cat Scene
Investigators, but no new cases had come up
lately. Bucky claimed that Elvis was an
expert on dogs too. He liked bragging about
Elvis's IQ, claiming he was as smart as
Albert Einstein.

Elvis was a little kid with skin as black as
pitch. He wore a pair of gigantic looking red
rim glasses reminding me of that little
egghead chicken on the cartoons. I have
never seen so many pockets in my life as he
had in the clothes he wore. Every one of
them concealed mysteries and magical
contraptions, something for every occasion
or crisis. He didn't speak like a kid. I guess
his IQ was to blame.

Bucky was what Papa called big boned. He
had a round face. As a matter of fact, most
everything about Bucky was round. He was
twice the size of Elvis and they were
supposed to be the same age. Daddy said
Bucky was big for his age and Elvis way too
small for his. I guess that put me in the 'just

right' category because my size matched neither of them.

I could tell by the serious look on Elvis's face that something troubling was heading my way. He squinted while rubbing his chin, all the while looking at Getouttahere. My dog stared back at Elvis, tail wagging slowly, his head cocking one way and then the other. The two of them knew something that neither Bucky nor I apparently knew.

"Where did you acquire your domesticated carnivorous mammal?" asked Elvis.

"My what," I asked him.

"Your highly variable domestic mammal, *Canis familiaris,* a family of mammals, including dogs, jackals, wolves, and foxes, typically having a bushy tail, erect ears, and a long muzzle, order *Carnivore,* belonging to the *Canidae* but yours does not have these traits. It seems more hybrid than typical."

"He's talking about your pooch, Tyler. He just says it different than most. He can't help it talking over our heads I'm afraid. I've been told that it has to do with his IQ number. It makes him talk over our heads sometimes."

"Papa said he is a stray, just wandered into the yard and I kept him. He's what Papa calls a sooner."

"I almost met a stray dog once. Me, Cole Brown and Stanton Paul had surrounded a mangy long-haired mutt and we all wanted him. Cole came up with this way to decide which one of us would take him home. He said the one that could tell the best lie won him. Before we could get to it, Preacher Watters butted in and asked us what we were doing to the poor dog. Cole up and told him that the best liar among us would get the dog. Preacher Watters told us it wasn't God's will for any of us to go around telling lies. He said he never lied when he was our age. Cole gave him the dog for being the best liar."

"You made that up, Bucky."

"Well if I did, do I get your sooner then, Tyler?"

Unfazed by his cousin's babbling, Elvis set the record straight. "Many dogs are not purebred but are rather a mix of two or more breeds. These dogs are sometimes also referred to as mutts or Heinz 57. Some dogs have been given new breed names that are a combination of the two parent breeds. For example, a Boggle is a Boxer and Beagle mix, while a Yorkie-Poo is a Yorkshire Terrier and Poodle mix, a complete mix containing parts of many different origins."

"That would be my dog, Getouttahere."

"Get out of here. We just got here. That's kind of rude, don't you think?"

"Bucky, Getouttahere is my dog's name."

"How original," added Elvis.

"You call your dog Getouttahere. How do you get him to come to you?"

"Come now, Bucky, obviously this dog must be extremely intelligent to overcome such obstacles that would send any other breed scurrying as scolded."

I asked Elvis did he know about scolding dogs.

Bucky answered for him. "My cousin knows about everything I keep telling you, cats, dogs, how to make peanut butter and banana sandwiches, the universe and beyond."

Elvis then said, "Just how intelligent is your dog, that's the 'inquiring minds want to know' question. Dog breeds have been ranked in order of intelligence. Stated from

1 to 10 with 1 being the smartest, Border Collie, Poodle, German Shepherd, Golden Retriever, Doberman Pinscher, Shetland Sheepdog, Labrador Retriever, Papillon, Rottweiler and Australian Cattle Dog."

"Sorry Tyler, he didn't mention sooner, mutts or Heinz 57."

"Maybe my dog is a mixture of several of those smart dogs."

"Anything is possible. Perhaps we should test your canine phoneme."

"There's a test for telling how smart a dog is, Elvis?"

"Can he fetch stuff, sit up and rollover or play dead?" asked Bucky.

"It's a bit more to it than simple tricks, Bucky." Elvis retrieved a notepad, pencil and stopwatch from various pockets. He then asked me to fetch a towel, smiling at his attempt at sarcasm. Test one would require that we toss a towel over Getouttahere's head and using the stopwatch, time how long it would take for him to get free. First, Elvis allowed his test specimen to smell the mauve towel with lace trim, snuck from the main bathroom. Elvis explained the scoring 30 seconds or less, 3 points, 31 to 120 seconds, 2 points, tries but doesn't succeed within 120 seconds, 1 point, doesn't try, 0 points. He tabulated the score in his notepad after examining the time on the stopwatch. He didn't share the results.

Next, he would hide a doggie treat under the towel, one he so happened to have in one of those pockets. First, he allowed the canine to sniff the reward. As Getouttahere watched, he then placed it on the floor and covered it with the fancy towel. He started the stopwatch to time how long it would take the dog to reach the treat. Similar scoring applied to exercise number two. Elvis again recorded the results without revealing them to us.

Elvis set up the next test, saying, "Test number three will require a gap low to the ground, one that the canine can reach with its paws but not its muzzle. A couch would work if we had one. We could make one out of a pair of books and a wide wooden plank. We weigh down the top of the plank so your dog can't easily knock it over. I'll then place a treat underneath the plank while your dog is watching, pushing it far enough underneath so he can't reach it with its muzzle. You then encourage your dog to get the treat while I time it."

"The next test is designed to challenge a dog's memory, not its problem-solving skills. To do this, your dog needs to understand what's going on. We place a treat underneath a plastic cup and then you tell your dog to find it. Lift the cup to show him where it is. Do this about nine or ten times until he learns that treats go underneath cups. We then place three plastic cups upside down on the floor, a foot apart. We put a treat underneath one of the cups while your dog is watching. You then lead your dog out of the room for 30 seconds and then back. Urge him to find the treat while I time him. I have another treat if you can supply the three cups."

All tests had been completed. Elvis meticulously tabulated the scores, scrunching up his face and blinking rapidly as he analyzed the results. He took a deep breath, adjusted the glasses on his nose before sharing the score with us.

"Your dog scored as follows. He worked his way from the towel tossed over his head in 14 seconds for 3 points. He located the treat underneath the towel in 9 seconds for additional 3 points. Your dog was able to reach the treat underneath the plank using its paws in less than a minute for 4 points. Last test, he found the treat underneath the correct cup on his first attempt for 2 points.

A dog scoring 0 total points has the intelligence of a mop. A total score of between 1 and 3 points indicates your dog is a certified barker, not a thinker. An average dog would score between 4 and 7 points. Scoring 8 to 10 points would signify a dog was an obedience school honor student. Mister Getouttahere scored a whopping 12 points making him a canine genius, anything scored as high as 11 or 12 points."

"How about that, Tyler, your dog is as smart as Elvis."

"My IQ is 170. He scored a 12 on the dog scale. The correlation is not that simple."

"Maybe I should have named him Einstein instead."

With that, Getouttahere pressed his nose firmly against one of Elvis's pockets and then barked three times. Elvis turned his pocket inside out dumping the contents in his hand, three dog treats. Getouttahere gobbled them from his palm. We busted a gut laughing.

"Come Bucky, we have an appointment. Something has been digging complex burrowing systems below ground in Pastor Quinn's vegetable garden. It has my investigative juices flowing."

"It wasn't Getouttahere. I don't think he knows how to dig complex burrows."

"Don't shortchange him, Tyler. You heard Elvis's test results. Your dog has the smarts from a bunch of breeds. He's not a regular A1."

"It's Heinz 57, Bartholomew Owens. Quicken your steps. The pastor is not a patient man."

"And I'm going as quickly as I can. See you later Tyler."

"Later, Bucky…"

If you want the best seat in the house move the dog.

One of Papa's favorite things to do is sitting in one of his porch rockers watching the world pass by while chewing the fat. I'm not sure I get the chewing the fat part, but I usually sit in the other rocker looking for whatever we're supposed to be watching for in the world. It's for the men folk so says Papa, a time dedicated to men discussing manly topics.

Hunting and fishing top the discussions most of the time. Today it was Papa and me time. I was ill prepared for what subjects might be explored. Papa never hinted to what we might be covering. He called it 'off the cuff', being spontaneous and just speaking one's mind. One thing for sure, he always spoke his.

He asked me how my flea biter was doing, one of his names for Getouttahere. He never called my dog by the name I named him. You'd think he would since he was sort of responsible for me naming him what I named him. Getouttahere stretched out on the porch beside my rocker, flopped over on his side. His tail would wag if his name was mentioned. Flea biter didn't prompt a tail wag though. Papa called him other names but with the same results, no results whatsoever. My dog appreciated being called what he was supposed to be called, not made up names.

Papa believes dogs tend to occupy unoccupied space and mostly space being the space that people desire to occupy. Good for nothing hounds have this natural ability to aggravate the hands that feed them, so says Papa. It's instinctive in the canine genes, something that goes back to when they were ancient wolves. He really talks above my head a lot of the time.

I've learned to just nod and not ask questions. Asking questions prompt more answers than I am bargaining for, so I leave well enough alone. Papa tended to be a stickler for these lazy good for nothing dog conversations. I don't think he really meant to hurt me or my dog, it's just his way.

He told me to sit back and observe. I nodded. Papa then motioned for me to come with him. I did what he asked me to do. We had a seat in the porch glider, the one with padded cushions. Getouttahere followed us and sat down beside me, looking up at me, tongue and tail wagging. I patted him on the head, and he stretched out beside me. We rocked in the glider for a spell.

Papa eventually nudged me and winked, then motioned for me to follow him. We went inside. I almost asked him why we had but thought better of it. He read my mind and told me to be patient. Patience isn't something kids are that good at, better suited for being fidgety instead. I did my best to be patient in a fidgety sort of way.

I'm not sure how long we stayed inside. I don't have a watch, but Papa does. He pulled the chain from his front overall pocket until the round watch at the end of the chain was in the palm of his hand. It's called a pocket watch for that reason I suppose. He nodded this time and placed it back in his pocket.

Papa then walked over to the screen door. I followed. He didn't tell me to follow him but I just figured it out on my own. Papa says men have an unspoken bond, something understood between kin and friends. I'm both, so it must be really powerful between us.

I stopped just behind him. He was staring out the door. He grunted and then stepped out from in front of me so that I could see what he was looking at out there. I wasn't sure what he wanted me to see until he grabbed me by the back of my head and pointed me to where he wanted me to look.

There, curled up in the glider was
Getouttahere. Papa then went on to explain
that the flea-bitten squatter knew we'd be
coming back and now occupied our space.
Point proven, I couldn't dispute the evidence
Papa had presented.

He said it was an open and closed case, dog
guilty as charged. I didn't even know my
dog had been put on trial. Papa told me to
think about it; how many times had I seen
my hound do the same thing at home. I
hadn't really thought about it, so I gave it a
think and sure enough, I had seen
Getouttahere do this.

Nothing made my daddy madder than my
dog getting in his favorite chair. Daddy had
this tan leather recliner that he said was his
sitting place directly in front of the
television set. He didn't take too kindly to
others sitting there, even family and visiting
company. I had never thought much about it
before now, but Daddy occupied his very
own space, something not offered up to
others and especially not my dog.
Getouttahere didn't know any better.
According to Papa, he really did though.
Guilty as charged again, so pointed out
Papa.

Mama's hackles got bristled when
Getouttahere climbed atop a freshly made

bed. She said he waited until she had washed and changed the bed linens to curl up on my bed and sometimes theirs. He wasn't too picky where. Cleanliness is close to Godliness is what I remember somebody saying, not that I really knew what that saying meant.

Luckily Daddy never caught him doing this or my dog would have never set paws inside the house again. I reckon Papa had made his point. The best seat in the house or on the porch is always occupied by the dog. I wondered if Getouttahere had learned it somewhere else before arriving here or if it was a natural ability like Papa said it was.

Chasing your tail gets you nowhere except back to where you started.

Papa used to always accuse me of chasing my tail. He'd say, 'boy, you'll run yourself ragged running in those big ole circles.' I just laughed at him when he said a lot of the stuff he said, not to be mean but because I didn't always understand what he meant. Sometimes he explained it but most of the time he didn't. He said part of growing up you were supposed to figure things out on your own. I sure did my fair share of figuring as a kid. Figuring out what my new dog was up to kept me very busy too. I didn't always have Papa around with his abundance of wisdom. That was okay. I had the next best thing, Elvis the boy genius.

If ever I was confused, concerned or in just one of my trying to figure out stuff modes, Elvis had this uncanny ability to sense it and drop in out of nowhere. Maybe geniuses are smart that way. Elvis has one of those extra senses or something. Bucky tagged along to toss in his two cents worth. Wisdom oddly has no boundaries.

Getouttahere sometimes chased his tail and for the life of me I couldn't figure out why he did this. He'd be fine one minute and then running in circles like a twirling top. It made be quite dizzy watching his antics. I was going to ask Papa about it but that's when Elvis and Bucky magically appeared in my backyard. They seemed to do that a lot, genius and…well…Bucky.

"What's wrong with your dog, Tyler?"

"I'm not sure, Bucky. He does this sometimes for reasons I can't figure out."

"Canine behavioral disorders are not uncommon."

Bucky rolled his eyes. "Here we go. Mister Know-it-all has an answer for everything. It's my cousin's IQ curse. I'm sure glad it doesn't run in the family. I'm not cursed that way."

"Elvis, do you know why Getouttahere chases his tail?"

"There are many rhymes to the reasons, Tyler. We can explore them and possibly determine the root cause of your canine's antics."

"That would be terrific. If we can figure out why he does it, maybe we can find a way to stop him from doing it."

"Often the dog will engage in tail-chasing because they are merely bored. It's a way for them to have fun and expend some energy. This is especially true for puppies, who may not even realize that their tail is actually a part of their body but see it as a toy."

"Getouttahere isn't exactly a puppy and how can I tell if he's bored?"

"Tyler, older dogs become bored, not so much pups. I don't see yours as one that might be bored. You and he seem to stay quite active. I think we can rule this one out." Elvis handed Bucky a notepad and instructed him to take notes. Bucky took the pad and pencil but never understood just exactly what his cousin wanted him to write in it.

"Anxiety is another possible cause."

"How do you spell that, Elvis?"

Elvis ignore Bucky and continued, "Stress, fear of separation or even thunderstorms can cause one to suffer anxiety."

"I sure hate thunderstorms. They make me right stressful, but I can't recall every chasing my tail during one of those thunder clappers."

"This doesn't apply to you, Bucky."

"Nope, thunder and lightning don't seem to bother Getouttahere."

"What about fleas? Maybe he has fleas and all that whirling around is his way of shedding them. They end up on the tip of his tail before he flings them off. They hang on for as long as they can. Maybe that's why he doesn't do it all the time; only when he has a bunch of biting fleas causing that anxiety thing. Then once they are gone, he gets bored and stops."

Elvis had all the answers, even for his cousin. "Well, Bucky, something as simple as fleas or an itching rash could be a symptom but let's explore all the possibilities first."

Bucky nodded. "F-l-e-a-s, fleas, I wrote it down just in case,"

"Might your canine be frustrated, Tyler?"

"Frustrated at what?"

Á dilemma he can't resolve…"

"How do you spell die-limb-uh?"

"Do you keep him confined to a crate or inside a fence?"

"He stays in my bedroom, but I don't shut or lock the door."

"Let's rule that one out for now then."

Bucky sighed. "Good, I didn't know how to spell it anyway."

"Could be that he is conflicted."

"Convicted of what?"

"Not convicted, conflicted, Bucky. Maybe he wants to do one thing but thinks Tyler doesn't want him to do it."

"Like chasing his tail. Tyler doesn't want him doing that, Elvis."

"Getouttahere does most anything he wants to do. I never learned how to scold him properly."

"I wish my mama hadn't learned how. She's really good at it and she practices it a lot on me, doesn't she, Elvis?"

"Compulsive disorder, some dogs as well as people just have quirky habits they can't seem to help."

"That would be mama and her scolding. Sometimes she makes me go out in the yard and pick a switch off the tree. Her scolding can turn to much worse ways if I don't mind her like she thinks I should be minding her. I try to take my scolding like a man to avoid all that other stuff."

"Bucky, please stop disrupting me with your personalization of the issues."

"I can't even begin to start spelling that last word, so I'll just write down out of order like you said in the first place."

"Disorder…" Elvis corrected him.

"This order, that order, just help Tyler and his dog's tail-chasing trouble, Elvis"

"Genetics, it could be that tail chasing runs in his particular breed. The problem, he's a Heinz 57, so we can't narrow it down to breed type."

"Steak sauce talk makes me hungry. Hurry up and figure this out, Elvis."

"We're not exactly getting anywhere, are we?"

"Patience, Tyler, an accurate diagnosis takes time. How often does he chase his tail?"

"I haven't been keeping count. He doesn't do it every day."

Bucky smiled and then said, "It must be fleas. Dip his tail in that flea medicine and I bet he quits."

"Has he ever actually caught and bitten his tail?"

"Nope, not that I've ever seen."

"Chasing one's tail might be no more than a silly habit, like biting fingernails or scratching an itch. I wouldn't worry too much about your canine acting in this manner. If he actually catches his tail, then we might have to reopen the case."

"I'd worry more about him catching a car," added Bucky. "My uncle had a German Shepard that chased cars and trucks. That poor dog stayed at the vet's getting patched up all the time. His teeth and tires didn't get along too good."

"I feel like we've been chasing our tails and we're right back where we started."

"Very well said, Tyler. Let me know if I can assist you in any other troubling matters. For now, we will be on our way. The neighborhood awaits us. There are others less fortunate that most certainly require my assistance."

"I'm hungry, Elvis. You can go solve the neighborhood's problems. I'm done chasing my tail for one day. I should write that down."

"Indeed, you should, cousin. Indeed, you should. A mind is a terrible thing to waste."

For whatever reason, Getouttahere never chased his tail again, not that I ever noticed. Possibly Elvis was some sort of dog whisperer was the best answer I could come up with, but what we did I know. I wasn't a genius like him.

Life is just one table scrap after another when please doesn't work ... Beg!

Dogs eat dog food. People eat people food, end of the story according to Papa. Once you feed a dog people food the dog will turn its nose up to dog food, so he warned me numerous times. He said meaty discarded bones didn't count. Dogs needed to chew on bones. It kept them from chewing on important stuff like leather shoes.

Dogs, especially puppies, will chew on most anything, like a cat using everything for a scratching post. Papa doesn't like cats either, except for those in his barn that eat other nuisance critters. Beggars can't be choosey, so never fall in the dog trap says Papa. A dog will snooker you every time if you let it.

My dog, Getouttahere, had an Elvis like IQ, so he was much smarter than the average dog. That worried me, having a dog possibly smarter than me. How could I tell if he was trying to snooker me? I don't think he has a dishonest bone in his body but being snookered sounds deceitful and downright sneaky to me.

Papa doesn't trust any dogs. Heck, Papa doesn't trust many people. He says being suspicious is a man's best virtue. It can head off a heap of trouble if you can weed out the

111

bad folks from the good folks in life. Without Elvis around for advice I guess I was going to have to lean on Papa and his way of thinking. Here goes.

I asked him how I could stop Getouttahere from begging before he learned how to beg. He did what he always does. He patted me on the head and then smiled at me. Lesson time was around the corner now. He asked me what I did when I walked into Granny's kitchen and smelled something that made me smack my lips. He said for me to think about her freshly baked homemade chocolate chip cookies. I smacked my lips just thinking about those cookies. He laughed saying the dog's nose smells stuff a hundred times better than ours.

Like me, a dog would drool when it smelled good cooking, hopeful that what it smelled was meant for it to eat. You can't blame the dog for liking what it smells but you can sure blame people for giving into the dog. You can't argue with fact, so says Papa. A dog will look at you with those pitiful eyes and snooker you into feeding it. You have to be smarter than that or you deserve what you get, a whiney beggar at the table come feeding time.

Okay, so I got that part of it, but how did I stop it from starting I asked him. One simple way, so he said, put the varmint outside before mealtime. He added that no dog had any business in the house in the first place, especially around the dinner table. Papa wasn't partial to animals inside the house, any animals. I had not made him happy bringing the common stray inside mine, but he had been the one that I had helped convince my folks to let my dog stay inside. It was forgetting that important fact. He should have told me about the begging part first. Hindsight, going to Elvis instead of Papa might have been my better choice. No turning back now. I stumbled deeper into Papa's world and his say so on the matter.

He told me best that I didn't look my dog in the eyes if I chose to let him stay in the house. Dogs can hypnotize you if you give them half the chance. Before you know it, you're tossing them a little nibble from your plate. He grunted, saying once you cross that fine line it's just a matter of time before you toss the mutt another and then another. Might as well pull the beggar up a chair and push a plate in front of him. I could tell just the mere mention of this angered Papa. Talking to Bucky even seemed a better idea given the look on Papa's face.

He told me that I should practice training myself first. I asked him what he meant. He said for me to practice looking away if I was determined not to put that dog outside where he belonged before meals. He warned me that human food didn't agree with a dog's fortitude. It would make mine fat and unhealthy. I sure didn't want to do that to Getouttahere. Fat dogs were more worthless in the long run.

Practice yelling 'no', a dog needs to understand the meaning of the word 'no.' I thought about how Papa had yelled at my dog the first time we had seen him, shouting for him to get out of the yard. That hadn't worked at all, but I decided to keep that thought to myself. Some things are better off not spoken. I had learned that from Papa too.

Don't get snookered if you yell 'no' and that dog just looks back at you and does nothing or even begins to whimper. I think Papa just remembered that first time in the yard. He said don't be taken in if my dog barks and places its paw on my leg. They can be very sneaky when they want what's on your plate, so he said.

Feeding him that first bite and you just rewarded bad behavior. Undoing it is tougher that allowing it to be done. Having a dog seemed to always come with more complications. Goldfish just stayed in a bowl and waited their turn to be fed. Frankie said I had over fed the fish. I sure didn't want to over feed my dog. Fat dogs have fat owners as I had recalled that previous lesson.

If the dog stayed in the house during meals, he warned me to never ever talk to my dog while at the table. That's like giving him an engraved invite. Never mention him by name. He again suggested just putting him outside, the easier row to hoe, so he framed it. Papa liked using gardening terms when he explained stuff to me. Row to hoe; I still didn't get it though.

One thing for sure, keeping Getouttahere from begging and eating from my plate rested solely on my young shoulders. Might be that I should let him outside before every meal, the easier so-called row to hoe if I'm understanding what Papa was trying to tell me. One thing for certain, Mama and Daddy wouldn't take too kindly to Getouttahere sniffing about the table while we were eating. A dog has the easy part. Kids have the tough part.

My dog Getouttahere never sniffed or begged at the table. He would just curl up at my feet and wait until the meal was over. My dog was a mixture of a lot of dogs but one of a kind in my book. The perfect dog even if Papa wouldn't admit it. Life is just one table scrap after another so he would say, whatever the heck that means. Grown-ups say things with meanings that don't mean anything to us kids. I reckon we're supposed to get it sooner or later once we're old enough to get it. I'm just glad Getouttahere has such a high IQ. He figures stuff out without me having to do things I don't really want to do. Another lesson learned, what can possibly be left?

You might be barking up the wrong tree if you think a barking dog never bites.

Bucky and Elvis, the former Cat Scene Investigators had dropped back over to Tyler's house, nothing better to do on this lazy summer afternoon. Getouttahere's barking alerted Tyler to their arrival. Bucky approached cautiously, unsure if the sooner would become an attack dog. The dog watched them approaching, the one good ear perked and tail wagging slowly.

Elvis eyed the canine, noting its detail as if seeing it for the first time. He scanned its markings, the yellowish fur accented by the large spot overlapping its midsection like a saddle, the single black left paw balanced by a black ring around its right eye.

"Not to worry," announced Elvis. "The canine recognizes us and isn't taking a threatening stance."

"How do you know this, Cousin?"

"It is okay boys. He's not going to bite you."

"As I stated, the canine's posture supports you fully, Tyler."

"Here we go, Mister Know-It-All, the amazing Elvis has an answer for everything."

"Please Bartholomew it is so unbecoming of you to display jealous tendencies. Don't fault me for having an IQ that exceeds most mere mortals. I consider it a gift that I must utilize to the utmost magnitude."

"Curse you mean; makes you talk gibberish to us mere mortals. We're kids, Elvis. We even act like kids. We like being kids. You've never been a kid, have you?"

"Childhood is highly overrated. There are far more important endeavors for those capable of understanding the true meaning of life."

"Come on guys. It's summer and we're out of school. It's a time for fun."

"Elvis's idea of fun is nothing like ours, Tyler. You know how he is."

"So, Elvis, tell us how you knew Getouttahere wasn't going to bite either of you."

"My pleasure, Tyler. All dogs bark, howl or whine to some degree. Excessive barking can be a sign of behavior problems. Your canine does not display such behavior. These creatures bark to warn or alert, to display playfulness or excitement, to seek attention or when suffering anxiety. Yours merely alerted you when we were here."

"What if he had bitten one of us, Cousin? Dogs don't read and research stuff like you."

"Oh Bartholomew, ye of little faith; I must educate you to the behavioral signs of the canine species. You too might learn from my teachings, Tyler. Obviously, we have previously conducted appropriate intelligence tests of your animal and we have ascertained that he possesses exceptional superiority tendencies."

"We get it, Elvis. Getouttahere is a smart pooch. What does that have to do with him biting or not biting us? If I were a dog, I'd probably bite you just for the mere fact that you'd scare me with how you act. Sometimes you can be a little too creepy for your age."

"Your sarcastic humor is your best asset, Bartholomew."

"You with the brilliant IQ should know but how did you know Tyler's dog's barking wouldn't get us bitten?"

"Quite simple Dogs do bite for reasons that can be traced back to instinct and pack mentality. Puppies bite and nip on others of their species and humans as a means for exploring their environment and learning their place in the pack. Owners must show their puppies that mouthing, and biting are not acceptable by teaching them bite inhibition. Adult canines can be motivated to bite from fear or because they are being defensive. A canine will define what it perceives as its property, protecting its turf. A dog inflicted by sickness or pain might be prone to inflict a bite. Apex canine assert their dominance through barking and biting. These creatures still possess predatory instinct, thusly; biting is embedded in their primal brains."

"Elvis please speak kid language or at least try to clean it up so that we mere mortals can understand what the heck you're saying. In other words, how did you know Tyler's dog wasn't going to chomp on us?"

"First of all, it is important to know that any canine has the potential to become aggressive, regardless of breed or history. Canines with violent or abusive histories or those bred for aggressive tendencies are much more likely to exhibit aggressive behavior towards people or others of their species."

"How did you know? Simple question, Elvis?"

"Tyler's canine recognized us from our previous visit. His demeanor spoke volumes. Dogs are excellent observers, much better than most humans, those not possessing exceptional IQs. Our posture, head carriage, gaits, and of course facial expressions speak volumes about our mood and motivation. Act happy and your canine will wag excitedly and present their favourite toy for you to toss. Hang your head in sorrow and your pet will slink over and affectionately press its head in your lap."

"I didn't feel particularly happy or sad when we arrived."

"Canines are especially adept at reading facial expressions."

"This is my regular face. I wasn't making any faces."

"Tyler, please attempt this mirroring experiment. Sit facing your canine and make an exaggerated happy face. Your canine will light up as well: big grin, relaxed ears, open facial expression."

I gave it a try. Bucky mimicked as best he could, standing directly behind me. Getouttahere indeed reacted as Elvis had described, the broken ear more relaxed than the good ear.

"Tyler, now furrow your brow and look stern. Your canine will recoil, avert its eyes, and look guilty as charged."

I did and Getouttahere again mimicked Elvis's reactive description. Bucky shook his head in disbelief.

"A canine's understanding of body language explains their uncanny ability to find the one person in the room who doesn't like dogs. A fearful person tends to tense up and stare. This immediately puts a dog on the defensive."

"I get it. Getouttahere could sense you boys as friends then."

"Canines also rely on sounds and smells, both senses much keener than ours. They understand voice tone and smell fear, anxiety or a threat."

"But we didn't say anything, and I had my bath last night, so I couldn't have stunk. I didn't feel afraid or any of the stuff you just said. Did you have a bath last night, Elvis?"

"I'm obsessive-compulsive about cleanliness but cleanliness has nothing to do with what I was attempting to explain."

"Dogs smell other dogs rear ends so there must be something to it."

"Bartholomew, just accept that Tyler's canine perceived us as no threat and most certainly recognized us as friend, not a foe and let's please move on. Your persistence is tiring me. You're barking up the proverbial wrong tree."

"What?"

"Tyler, I fear we have overextended our visit. Perhaps we should exit the premises and allow you enough time to overcome my cousin's zealous approach to life. Please don't hesitate to contact me if you require further analytical assistance."

"Thanks Elvis, I think. See you later Bucky."

"Let us know if Getouttahere goes missing or something. We're much better at investigating and solving missing pet mysteries than explaining how to do complicated stuff."

"Will, do Bucky."

**Dogs are not our whole life
but they make our lives whole.**

Papa had given in to me that day while we sat on his front porch. He had allowed his grandboy to take in the sooner that had wandered into his yard despite how hard he had tried to make the good for nothing trespasser run away. Granny told me once that it was destiny that Getouttahere came into my life. She firmly believes all things happen for a reason. Papa calls it a bunch of poppycock, saying no mangy dog just moseys into his yard with a purpose to be a friend to man or boy. Accidents don't happen with purpose. They are just accidents. Dogs need to have a purpose and shouldn't be freeloaders.

Like I've said before, Papa really likes my dog, but he is too stubborn to ever honestly admit it. That's okay too. He does a lot of neat stuff and never takes the credit for it or in his words 'owns up to it.' I'll cut him some slack. He's sure cut me plenty.

Having a dog, just any dog, might have been just fine, but I agree with Granny. Getouttahere showed up in mine because he was supposed to be my very best friend. A boy needs a dog or so said somebody. I don't remember who. In this case I think a special dog needed his very own boy and he chose me. I didn't go off looking for a dog nor had I really given it a whole lot of thought.

Yep, all things happen for a reason. It was meant to be, me and Getouttahere. Granny is a wise woman, just like Papa is a wise man. They are just wise differently. And, thanks to Elvis, I now know I have a wise dog. Wisdom seems to run in my family, two legged and four-legged kind. I sure hope I hold up to the real smart bargain. No one tested me to see if I had a high IQ. Maybe I'll ask Elvis the next time Bucky and he drop by for a visit.

It's odd how having a dog makes you feel so good. I don't look at it like most, thinking I own Getouttahere. The saying, man's best friend, doesn't imply ownership but instead friendship. Best friends can be dog and boy, right? It sure can't be Papa and dog, not something he'd ever admit anyway.

Elvis just the other day quoted a man named Will Rogers who said, 'If there are no dogs in Heaven, then when I die, I want to go where they went.' I like that saying. Bucky told me that if I didn't mind throwing balls to my dog for eternity then heaven probably had a spot for me and Getouttahere. Bucky always tries to outdo his cousin, even if he must make up stuff.

I still can't help wondering if my dog once lived with another boy or even a girl. He wasn't just some regular stray, even Papa said that. This dog had been with people. Some one may have mistreated him, and he ran away, but why did he like being around people if people had done him wrong.

Papa often says you can't solve all the mysteries of the universe or there would be no mysteries to keep us guessing. Still, I wish I knew where my dog had lived before he showed up in Papa's yard. I don't even know how old he is or when to celebrate his birthday.

What I do know is that **Getouttahere** makes me happy. It is hard to even think about my life without him. He taught me almost everything I learned about taking care of him. I say almost only because my friends and family helped too. I would have never known how smart he was or about his behavioral stuff if not for Elvis.

Papa taught me a lot too but with Papa you must take what he calls 'everything with a grain of salt.' Papa sure tells me a lot of stuff that makes me think or just scrunch up my face trying to figure out what he is trying to make me think about. Having a dog doesn't take much thinking though.

Getouttahere makes me a happy boy. My worst fear, somebody will show up and claim I have their dog.

Papa says possession is nine tenths of the law. I asked him what that meant. He told me it was just a saying meaning that owning my dog is easier to do since I already do and not so easy to do if I didn't already have him. I reckon I understand what he's saying. Somebody would have to prove my dog is theirs. What if somebody did show up to claim him and Getouttahere recognized them and went directly over to them. What would that mean for possession of him? Like Papa says, we'll cross that bridge when we have to cross it. For now, we are best buddies and we will always be best buddies.

"Come here, Getouttahere, it's time you and me to be headed back home."

"Dogs are not our whole life, but they make our lives whole." Roger A. Caras

About T. Allen Winn

Winn began writing in 2003 while being cooped up in hotels during business travel. Ole T doesn't write under any specific genre. He writes what strikes his fancy. If you don't see something that fits your reading wheelhouse just tell him what you like, and he might just write it for you.

Books are available on Amazon or online where books are sold. Select books are available at Southern Succotash on Washington Street in Abbeville, S.C. and in Tabor City, N.C. at Grapefull Sisters Vineyard. Or *Message* T. Allen Winn on Facebook to arrange delivery of signed copies.

Fiction from T. Allen Winn

The Detective Trudy Wagner series

Road Rage
North of the Border
Tithes and Offerings

Foot Series

Foot, Tree Knockers and Rock Throwers
Another Foot, What Really Happened to D.
B. Copper?

More Fiction from T. Allen Winn

The Perfect Spook House
Dark Thirty
Lou Who
Raw Ride, a Wild West Zombie Apocalyptic
Shoot'um Up
The Man Who Met the Mouse
Mister Twix Mystery, a Cat Scene
Investigation
Come Here Getouttahere, Tyler's Tail
Wagging Tale
The Tenth Elemental
The Lord's Last Acres

Non-Fiction from T. Allen Winn

Being Bentley, A Dog Like No Other
It's All About the 'A', Faith, Family,
Football and Forever to Thee
with coauthor, Benji Greeson
It's All About the Angels in the Backfield,
Dawn of a Dynasty
with coauthor, Benji Greeson
December's Darkest Day, While I Breathe,
I Hope
The Hardwood Walker of Port Harrelson
Road (based on true events
in Bucksport, S.C.)
Cuz, My Brother, Life is Good, God is Good

Memoirs

The Caregiver's Son,
Outside the Window Looking In
Cornbread and Buttermilk, Good Ole
Fashion Home Cooked Nostalgic Nonsense
The Endless Mulligan, Short Shots
from the Golf Whomper
Don't Sit Naked in a Grits Tree, More
Nostalgic Nonsense Vol 2

Short Stories

For Your Amusement featured in Beach
Author Network's book titled 'Shorts'

Ciled Me a Bar featured in friend and
author, Danny Kuhn's Headline Book's
Mountain Mysts. It received honorable
Mention in Fiction at the 2015 London Book
Festival and the book is endorsed by *Joyce
Dewitt* of the sitcom *Three's Company*

Short story about Granny Bowie in friend
and author Robert Sharpe's book, *The Heart
and Soul of Caring*, about caregivers and
their challenges

www.ingramcontent.com/pod-product-compliance
Lightning Source LLC
Chambersburg PA
CBHW032038040426
42449CB00007B/939